Galatians

A Digest of Reformed Comment

Galatians

A Digest of Reformed Comment

GEOFFREY B. WILSON
MINISTER OF BIRKBY BAPTIST CHURCH
HUDDERSFIELD

THE BANNER OF TRUTH TRUST

THE BANNER OF TRUTH TRUST
3 Murrayfield Road, Edinburgh EH12 6EL
P.O. Box 621, Carlisle, Pennsylvania 17013, USA

*

© *1979 Geoffrey Backhouse Wilson*
First published 1979
ISBN 0 85151 294 1

*

Printed in Great Britain by
Hazell Watson & Viney Ltd
Aylesbury, Bucks

TO SARAH, STEPHEN
PAUL AND RACHEL

CONTENTS

PREFACE

I am again indebted to the authors and publishers without whose generous co-operation this book could not have appeared, and to the Evangelical Library and Dr Williams's Library for the loan of various books. In recent times no one has recaptured the spirit of Galatians so well as J. Gresham Machen, and this revised edition reflects the help I have received from his inspiring but, alas, incomplete Notes on the Epistle. The commentary is based on the American Standard Version (1901), published by Thomas Nelson Inc., and chapter summaries have been added.

Huddersfield
February 1979

GEOFFREY WILSON

INTRODUCTION

The identity of the Galatians is a relatively modern problem, for among ancient interpreters it was universally assumed that they were a people of Celtic descent who lived in that part of Asia Minor which once formed the old kingdom of Galatia. But it is doubtful whether Paul penetrated so far north as Ancyra (now Ankara), Tavium, or even Pessinus, and we have no record that any churches were founded in those regions. Most scholars therefore now think, thanks largely to the work of Sir William Ramsay, that Paul uses the term to designate the existing Roman province of Galatia, which included those towns in the south which he and Barnabas had visited on the first missionary journey [*Acts* 13-14].

If this view, commonly known as the South Galatian theory, is accepted it becomes possible to date the letter before the Council of Jerusalem [*Acts* 15]. It is suggested that Paul wrote it either on his return to Syrian Antioch, or even perhaps while actually *en route* to the Council in AD 48 or 49. This would make the Epistle to the Galatians the earliest of Paul's extant letters, and it is not without significance that its theme is in complete harmony with the principle so boldly enunciated in his first sermon to the Galatians at Pisidian Antioch [*Acts* 13.38, 39]. The advantage of adopting this early date is that by identifying *Galatians* 2.1ff with the 'famine relief visit' of *Acts* 11.27-30 rather than with Paul's attendance at the Council, it avoids the difficulty of explaining why he did not appeal to a decision which would have settled the point at issue in the Galatian churches [*Acts* 15.19–29]. With his customary acumen Calvin regarded this difficulty as the conclusive reason for maintaining that the Epistle was written before that Council was held.

Thus we arrive at the following probable sequence of events. When Paul had worked with Barnabas for about a year in Antioch [*Acts* 11.26], they were commissioned by the church there to carry the famine relief fund to Jerusalem. In the course of this visit the Jerusalem apostles fully recognized that Paul and Barnabas had a divine vocation to take the gospel to the Gentiles [*Gal* 2.1–10]. Some time later they were sent out by the church at Antioch on the first Gentile mission during which they established churches at Pisidian Antioch, Iconium, Lystra, and Derbe. Shortly after their return to Syrian Antioch, the misguided enthusiasm for the law shown by certain emissaries from the Jerusalem church caused a breach in table-fellowship between Jewish and Gentile believers so that even Peter and Barnabas no longer deemed it expedient to eat with the Gentiles. Although in itself this seemed a small matter, Paul had no hesitation in publicly opposing such a separation, for he could see that nothing less than the gospel was at stake [*Gal* 2.11–14]. As if this were not enough, Paul now learned that Judaizers had also appeared among his recently won converts in Galatia demanding their submission to all the requirements of the law including circumcision. In the Galatian Epistle Paul personally combats this subversive teaching, and not long afterwards the Council of Jerusalem officially outlawed it, but to win the victory over legalism was to cost the apostle a life-long struggle against these 'zealots for the law', whose ubiquitous activities threatened to stifle the faith of the infant church.

Of the Epistle's importance there is happily no doubt whatever, for as Luther so rightly insisted, the mastery of its message is basic to a true understanding of the Christian faith. In this brief letter there is distilled for us the quintessence of Paul's gospel. Here we are brought face to face with a man whose burning words express the measure of his care for the purity of that gospel and for the safety of his readers. And in days of widespread doctrinal decline we would do well to remember that there can be no genuine pastoral concern for the souls of men without a similar zeal to maintain and defend 'the faith which was once for all delivered unto the saints' [*Jude* 3].

CHAPTER ONE

In this letter Paul's salutation is notable for the omission of his customary thanksgiving, and for the emphasis he places on the divine commissioning which made him an apostle of God's grace [vv 1–5]. He at once expresses his surprise that the Galatians are so quickly deserting the truth for the false gospel of the Judaizers, and twice pronounces his solemn anathema on anyone who preaches another gospel [vv 6–9]. As Christ's servant, he is no man-pleaser since he received neither the gospel nor his office from men, but immediately from God [vv 10–12]. He could receive nothing from Christians before his conversion, because his zeal for the traditions of the fathers made him a bitter persecutor of the church. And when it pleased God to reveal his Son in him, he did not seek the approval or advice of the Jerusalem apostles, but went to Arabia and Damascus [vv 13–17]. When he visited Jerusalem three years later, he had stayed a fortnight with Peter, but did not then meet any other apostle except James the Lord's brother. And his subsequent departure for Syria and Cilicia meant that he had no personal contact with the Christians of Judæ, who nevertheless glorified God for turning their former persecutor into a preacher of the gospel [vv 18–24].

V1: Paul, an apostle (not from men, neither through man, but through Jesus Christ, and God the Father, who raised him from the dead),

Paul, an apostle (not from men, neither through man,

As the Judaizers had discredited Paul's teaching and gained the ear of the Galatians for their false gospel by denying the divine origin of his apostleship, this fiery letter to his fickle converts aptly begins with an emphatic assertion of the unique authority of his commission. With his third word, 'not', he launches into his sustained polemic. His calling was neither from men as an *ultimate* nor through man as a *mediate* authority, for no human source or agency could have given him that infallible authority which was his as an apostle of Christ. Mere men cannot make an apostle, and no human representative can convey the grace and gifts which the office demands. This is sufficient to explode the myth of apostolic succession so carefully cherished by the Papacy, since 'it is the property of an Apostle to be called immediately by Jesus Christ, hence it follows, that the authority, office, and function of Apostles ceased with them, and did not pass by succession to any other' (William Perkins).

but through Jesus Christ, and God the Father, The fact that a single preposition ('through') is here used to govern both nouns indicates that Paul conceived of Jesus Christ and God the Father as together sustaining the one supreme source of his apostolic authority. No higher source of authority could be envisaged, while all thought of any lower intermediary is ruled out.

who raised him from the dead), The exceptional character of his ministry was born of this conviction which had been indelibly stamped upon his heart by that divine encounter on the road to Damascus. 'As surely as God the Father had raised His Son Jesus from the dead and given Him glory, so surely had the glorified Jesus revealed Himself to Saul His persecutor to make him His Apostle' (G. G. Findlay). Thus it was by the sheer supernaturalism of his calling that he differed from the rest of the apostles. For they were appointed by Christ during the time of his humiliation, whereas Paul had received his commission from the exalted and glorified Christ.

*V*2: **and all the brethren that are with me, unto the churches of Galatia:**

The brethren who are with Paul as he writes were evidently his fellow missionaries. They share in full measure his anxiety to recover the Galatians from their apostasy. He says '*all* the brethren' to express their unanimity in the faith, yet avoids naming them in case his readers should think that the validity of his message depended upon their support. And it is in keeping with his insistence upon the independence of his apostleship of men that he adheres to the first person singular throughout this letter [cf I *Thess* 1, 2: 'Paul and Silvanus and Timothy ... *we* give thanks to God']. The curtness of his address is remarkable and reflects his anger at their swift defection from the one true gospel. For though he still calls them 'churches', their corrupted faith is unworthy of any commendation. The plural shows that this was a circular letter, and according to the South Galatian theory (see Introduction), the churches to which it was sent were those at Pisidian Antioch, Iconium, Lystra, and Derbe.

*V*3: **Grace to you and peace from God the Father, and our Lord Jesus Christ,**

'In this Pauline greeting, "grace" designates the undeserved favour of God, and "peace" the profound well-being of the soul which is the result of it' (J. G. Machen). This characteristic salutation therefore served to remind these erring Galatians of what they once gladly confessed. Grace alone had given them peace with God, a peace which they had put at risk by their dangerous dalliance with legalism. For the compromise of grace always leads to the forfeiture of peace. Hence they must learn afresh that it took nothing less and required nothing more than the achievement of 'grace' so freely conferred upon the undeserving, to give the assurance of an interest in that 'peace' with God which was purchased by the blood of Christ [*Eph* 2.11–18].

from God our Father, and the Lord Jesus Christ, (ASV margin) The reading 'our' is probably to be preferred here [cf NIV]. Once again the use of a single preposition ('from') presents God the Father and Christ the Lord as the sole source of this 'grace' and 'peace'. This not only places them on the same plane of divine equality, but also underlines the fact that the knowledge of God as 'our' Father is inseparably conjoined with the redemptive mediation of the Lord Jesus Christ.

*V*4: **who gave himself for our sins, that he might deliver us out of this present evil world, according to the will of our God and Father:**

who gave himself for our sins, This unusual extension of the greeting is an arresting announcement of the theme of the Epistle and the purpose of the gospel. It was to save sinners that Christ freely gave himself up to the suffering and death of the cross. The magnitude of the sacrifice which our sins called forth manifests the supreme folly of looking elsewhere for their forgiveness. It is high time the Galatians made up their minds concerning the sufficiency of Christ's sacrifice to save them from their sins, and that without the addition of their obedience to the superseded rites of the Mosaic law. Paul would have them know that his gospel – the free justification of the sinner through Christ crucified – means nothing to those for whom it does not mean everything. For as there were no half-measures in the sacrificial self-giving of Christ, so there can be no half-hearted acceptance of the message of salvation [*Gal* 2.21; 3.1]. 'The Judaizers are dead and gone, but not the issue that they raised. Faith or works – that is as much as ever a living issue . . . Paul in Galatians was fighting the age-long battle of the Christian Church. "Just as I am, without one plea but that thy blood was shed for me" – these words would never have been written if the Judaizers had won' (de J. G. Machen, *The New Testament*, pp. 129–130).

to rescue us from the present evil age, (NIV) No mere pedlars of religious reforms could deliver mankind from its helpless bondage to the prince of darkness. It called for an Almighty Saviour to liberate those held captive by the entrenched powers of evil. As John Calvin says, this one word 'evil' is a thunderbolt which lays low all human pride. For 'apart from the renewal brought about by the grace of Christ, there is nothing in us but unmixed wickedness. We are of the world, and until Christ rescues us from it, the world reigns in us and we live unto it'. This rescue does not immediately remove believers from what is now an alien environment; it is rather a spiritual emancipation from any part in the curse, character, and condemnation that belongs to the present age [*John* 17.15; 1 *John* 2.15, 16]. Christ thus sacrificed himself for our sins, so that we might be rescued from our bondage to an evil world [cf 4.9; 5.1].

according to the will of our God and Father: There is nothing fortuitous in this deliverance because it is the historical outworking of the eternal purpose of him who is at once our God and Father. 'Therefore we have not been delivered by our own will or exertion [*Rom* 9.16] or by our own wisdom or decision; we have been delivered because God has had mercy on us and has loved us. As it is written in another passage [*John* 1.13]: "Who were born, not of blood nor of the will of the flesh nor of the will of man, but of God". It is by grace, then, and not by our merit that we have been delivered from this present evil world' (Martin Luther).

[19]

*V*5: **to whom** *be* **the glory for ever and ever. Amen.**

It is in this letter alone that Paul finds himself unable to add any word of thanksgiving for the faith of his readers [*v* 6]. Instead he concludes his greeting with a fervent ascription of praise to God for that glory which essentially belongs to him and which therefore must endure throughout the endless ages of eternity. By inviting the Galatians to join in this adoration, the final 'Amen' virtually becomes a summons to return to the faith from which they had so quickly declined.

*V*6: **I marvel that ye are so quickly removing from him that called you in the grace of Christ unto a different gospel; 7 which is not another** *gospel***; only there are some that trouble you, and would pervert the gospel of Christ.**

I am astonished that you are so quickly deserting him who called you in the grace of Christ and turning to a different gospel – not that there is another gospel, (RSV) Paul is amazed to learn that the Galatians are forsaking the gospel so quickly after their conversion. As he writes they are in the very act of turning from it, and the urgency of his address is dictated by the hope of bringing them to a better mind before the process of apostasy is complete. To recover them from the brink of spiritual disaster, it was necessary to show them the true nature of their defection. This was no less than a deserting of 'him' (the Galatians know very well that he means 'God') who is the author of that call which came to them through the preaching of the apostle. But the distinctive feature of the gospel which they had inexcusably overlooked is that this calling by God to salvation is ever and only 'in the grace of Christ'. Thus the essence of their folly was that they were guilty of 'abandoning the position of grace, i.e., the relation towards God which made them the objects of the grace of Christ and participators in its benefits, to put themselves under law, which could only award them their sad deserts' (Ernest De Witt Burton). They were forfeiting these inestimable privileges by turning to a *different* gospel. Such a gospel is really no gospel at all, for though it assumes the name of gospel it is so completely emptied of any power to save that it is of an entirely different kind from the one authentic gospel preached by Paul.

only there are some that trouble you, and would pervert the gospel of Christ. These Judaizers have successfully infiltrated the churches of Galatia by dignifying a different doctrine with the name of gospel, but to receive another gospel is to embrace another faith [2 *Cor* 11.4]. Although the Galatians have not yet succumbed to this false teaching, Paul lets them know that they are being confused and unsettled by those who wished so completely to change the character of Christ's gospel that it no longer belonged to him. Since 'the gospel preached by them was conformity to the Mosaic ritual, it was in antagonism to that gospel which has Christ for its theme, for by its perversion it would render "Christ of none effect". Whatever would derogate from the sufficiency of Christ's gospel, or hamper its freeness, is a subversion of it, no matter what guise it may assume, or how insignificant the addition or subtraction may seem' (John Eadie).

*V*8: **But though we, or an angel from heaven, should preach unto you any gospel other than that which we preached unto you, let him be anathema.**

But even if we, or an angel from heaven, should preach to you a gospel contrary to that which we preached to you, (RSV) As God is the author of the gospel, so gospel authority is never inherent but always derived. It is only as the messenger remains faithful to the divine message that he speaks with divine authority. Neither Paul nor his colleagues are free to alter the message they were commissioned to declare. Hence even if they, or indeed an angel from heaven itself, should present the Galatians with a gospel whose content was contrary to that which they had preached to them, they could not hope to escape the divine 'anathema'. The word literally means 'devoted', but it is used here in the bad sense of being devoted to destruction [cf *Deut* 7.26].

let him be accursed. (RSV) i.e. by God and as such rejected with abhorrence by all true believers. No words could more plainly exhibit the awful doom that must overtake anyone, whether apostle or angel, who takes it upon himself to preach as God's message of salvation what is in fact a complete perversion of the one true gospel. As no crime is worse than this, so no judgment is heavier. But this 'will not justify our thundering out anathemas against those who differ from us in lesser things. It is only against those who forge a new gospel, who overturn the foundation of the covenant of grace, by setting up the works of the law in the place of Christ's righteousness, and corrupting Christianity with Judaism, that Paul denounces this' (Matthew Henry).

*V*9: **As we have said before, so say I now again, If any man preacheth unto you any gospel other than that which ye received, let him be anathema.**

As we have said before, so say I now again, This is a reminder that they had been warned on a previous occasion against giving heed to false teaching, probably on his return visit when Barnabas was his companion [*Acts* 14.21ff]. 'It is therefore no surprise to Paul to learn, as he does now, that Judaistic propaganda is going on in Galatia: what does surprise him, as he says in verse 6, is that it is achieving so immediate and so signal a success' (G. S. Duncan).

If anyone is preaching to you a gospel contrary to that which you received, let him be accursed. (RSV) In passing from an improbable supposition [v 8] to a condition of reality, Paul does not shrink from applying the same divine sentence of condemnation to what is now actually taking place in Galatia. He might well marvel that they should be so willing to listen to a message which was a flagrant contradiction of the gracious good news they had heard and received from him. Only those who are blind to the glory of the gospel and the seriousness of the situation blame the apostle for the severity of his language. 'As there is only one God, so there can be only one gospel. If God has really done something in Christ on which the salvation of the world depends, and if He has made it known, then it is a Christian duty to be intolerant of everything which ignores, denies, or explains it away. The man who perverts it is the worst enemy of God and men' (James Denney, *The Death of Christ*, p. 66).

V10: **For am I now seeking the favour of men, or of God? or am I striving to please men? if I were still pleasing men, I should not be a servant of Christ.**

'For' advances the reason for this severity. Evidently the Judaizers had represented him as a man who had no scruples in relaxing what they regarded as the essential requirements of the gospel in order to gain Gentile converts more easily. But surely no one who is intent on currying favour with men approaches them with anathemas! Is the man who utters such strictures really the ingratiating compromiser his opponents make him out to be? Then let the Galatians acknowledge that he never seeks the favour of *men* at the cost of losing the approval of GOD. As Bengel tersely comments: 'Regard is to be had to God alone'.

if I were still pleasing men, I should not be a servant of Christ. If, while Paul claimed to be the bondservant of a

Master to whom he owed absolute obedience, he nevertheless sought to please men, his devotion to Christ would be no more real than the sham service of his accusers [cf 6.12, 13]. 'No one can serve Him who makes it his study to be popular with men. For to His servant His will is the one law, His work the one service, His example the one pattern, His approval the continuous aim, and His final acceptance the one great hope' (Eadie) [*Matt* 6.24].

*V*11: **For I make known to you, brethren, as touching the gospel which was preached by me, that it is not after man.**

In still addressing the erring Galatians as his 'brethren' (nine times in this Epistle), Paul appeals to that bond of union which was forged between them through the preaching and receiving of the gospel of God's grace. If he finds it necessary to 'make known' to them what they already know, it is because they are now listening to an entirely different message which has made them forget the distinctive character of this gospel. In contrast to those who had followed him, the gospel preached by Paul is not 'after man'. It was not invented or developed by man, but is as supernatural in its origin as it is in its effects [3.2]. 'It is above man's devising, to be received and handed on in its integrity, neither diminished nor increased' (A. Lukyn Williams).

*V*12: **For neither did I receive it from man, nor was I taught it, but *it came to me* through revelation of Jesus Christ.**

It would seem that the apostle's critics in Galatia had charged him with claiming an authority he did not possess, for they said that he preached only a garbled version of the gospel which he had received at second-hand. But Paul insists that his gospel was not 'from man', because it had not come to him through any human intermediary; it was neither transmitted by tradition, nor conveyed by instruction. On the contrary, the gospel came to Paul through the transforming experience of an immediate revelation of the Risen Christ. It was this divine disclosure which convinced the erstwhile persecutor that the object of his hatred had been none other than the Son of God himself! [*Acts* 9.5] Thus he received the gospel, of whom Christ is the sum and substance, and the commission to preach it, in that moment when his soul was illuminated by the blinding vision of his Conqueror [1.16].

*V*13: **For ye have heard of my manner of life in time past in the Jews' religion, how that beyond measure I persecuted the church of God, and made havoc of it:**

Paul's third 'for' [*vv* 10, 12] introduces evidence to prove that there was nothing in his former career which predisposed him towards the faith he now proclaimed. The Galatians had heard, probably in the first place from his own lips, of his boundless persecuting zeal against those whom he once regarded as the guilty followers of a blasphemous imposter, but who were in fact those whom he had come to recognize as the true people (*ekklēsia*) *of God*. Paul's use of the expression here shows that he had not only learned to think of each local assembly of believers as 'the church of God' in that particular place, but had also already learned to regard the entire body of believers as constituting the one universal church. Hence this was the term 'which came most naturally to his lips when he was speaking of his persecution of the Christians' (Burton). His application of this title to believers further shows that he already regarded them as the chosen people of God, and this indicates 'how fully, in his thought, the Christian church had succeeded to the position once occupied by Israel' (Burton). [cf 6.16]

Nothing short of a divine intervention could have turned such an audacious opponent into an outspoken champion of the faith he had tried so hard to destroy [*Acts* 8.3; 9.1, 13, 14; 22.4, 5; 26.10, 11]. The implied contrast between his former practice and his present faith is significant because it shows that Christianity was no offshoot of Judaism. The gospel he presented to the Galatians could not have sprung from the religion of petrified legalism he had renounced; it was the proper development of that Old Testament hope which was fulfilled in the Messiah whom Judaism had seen fit to reject.

*V*14: **and I advanced in the Jews' religion beyond many of mine own age among my countrymen, being more exceedingly zealous for the traditions of my fathers.**

This violent fanaticism was the expression of Paul's zeal for the traditions of Judaism, in devotion to which he outstripped all his contemporaries [*Phil* 3.4–6]. These traditions were those rules and regulations which purported to interpret the law of God, but which had really corrupted it into a crippling system of moral casuistry [cf *Matt* 5.21ff; 15.3, 6; 23.2ff]. Thus for as long as he followed the traditions of his fathers, he remained a stranger to Israel's ancestral *faith* and the avowed enemy of the Deliverer upon whom it was centred [4.4, 5]. When therefore conversion to Christ made so ardent a Jew as Paul break with this religion, how could the Gentile Galatians imagine that submission to its demands was necessary to complete the gospel?

*V*15: **But when it was the good pleasure of God, who separated me,** *even* **from my mother's womb, and called me through his grace, 16 to reveal his Son in me, that I might preach him among the Gentiles;**

As Bengel well says, 'The *good pleasure* of God is the farthest point which a man can reach, when inquiring as to the causes of his salvation'. Thus it was only when the time of God's antecedent purpose of grace was fulfilled that Paul was called to salvation and service. His furious career as a persecutor was then abruptly terminated and the whole course of his life entirely changed [*v* 16b.f]. The fact that Paul's calling meant a complete upheaval in his life sharply distinguishes him from the other apostles, who did not have to make such a radical break with their past. Moreover, they came to complete commitment to Christ 'only after much vacillation and a long course of instruction by Him. In the case of Paul we find no evidence of either vacillation or instruction' (K. Rengstorf, *TDNT*, Vol. I, p. 438). The apostle's affinity with Jeremiah probably here leads him consciously to adopt the prophet's language in describing his own call to service [cf *Jer* 1.5]. Paul is affirming his independence of men. His commission is neither derived from men nor subject to their control, for before he was even born God had set him apart to preach the gospel to the Gentiles!

to reveal his Son in me, There is always an *objective* element in revelation without which it would be nothing more than a formless mysticism. For Saul this was the real appearance of the Risen Christ on the Damascus road; for us it is the record of the same Christ as infallibly revealed in the inspired Scripture. But the *subjective* appropriation of this revelation of the Son of God always calls for the inward penetration of the Spirit. For 'no man can say that Jesus is Lord but by the Holy Spirit' [1 *Cor* 12.3]. Hence Paul does not merely say that it pleased God to reveal his Son 'to me' but '*in* me' [2 *Cor* 4.6].

that I might preach him among the Gentiles; The Christ who was privately revealed to Paul now had to be publicly proclaimed by him among the Gentiles. There is no preaching that is worthy of the name unless Christ is set forth in all the glory of his Person and all the fulness of his saving power. '*In this encounter with the person of the exalted Christ is to be found the starting point of Paul's apostolic preaching, as well as the real significance of his conversion, and it is this confrontation to which he appeals again and again to justify his preaching of Christ*' (Herman Ridderbos, *Paul and Jesus*, p. 46).

V16b: **straightway I conferred not with flesh and blood: 17 neither went I up to Jerusalem to them that were apostles before me: but I went away into Arabia; and again I returned unto Damascus.**

Having received such a revelation from *God*, Paul at once decided that he would not consult with mere 'flesh and blood', an expression emphasizing the weakness and frailty of *men*; 'whose intelligence is limited and their counsel moulded by the constitution of their material clothing' (J. A. Beet). Indeed so far was he from acknowledging any dependence upon the authority of the Jerusalem church that he did not even go to visit those who were, in point of time but not of standing, apostles before him. For what Paul needed was not conference with men but communion with God, and so after only a few days [cf *Acts* 9.19: 'certain days'] with the disciples in Damascus he travelled east to seek the solitude of the Nabatean desert. It is probable that his stay there was comparatively short, for on his return to Damascus he entered upon an extended period of evangelistic activity [*Acts* 9.20; cf *v* 23: 'many days'].

V18: **Then after three years I went up to Jerusalem to visit Cephas, and tarried with him fifteen days.**

Then The pointed repetition of this word draws attention to certain salient incidents which show the real nature of Paul's relations with the church in Jerusalem: 'his first introduction to them [*v* 18], his departure to a distant sphere of labour [*v* 21], and his return to Jerusalem with Barnabas [2.1]' (Frederic Rendall).

What Paul is concerned to stress is that it was not until *three years* after his conversion that he went up to Jerusalem to meet Peter with whom he spent *fifteen days*. After having exercised an independent commission for three years his visit was too late to seek Jerusalem's recognition of his calling, and it was too short for him to be looked upon as Peter's disciple. But the fact that Paul did not receive his *gospel* from an acknowledged superior does not mean that he failed to receive any part of the *gospel-tradition* from an honoured colleague. No doubt it was during this visit that he heard of the resurrection appearances to Peter and James from their own lips (cf F. F. Bruce, *Tradition Old and New*, p. 32). He makes no mention of the advocacy of Barnabas which secured this introduction, for it had no bearing on his inner convictions regarding the reality of his apostleship [cf *Acts* 9.26–29]. Paul's argument is that he 'enjoys the same apostolic authority as those who were apostles before him [*Gal* 1.17], because he, like them, received his commission and his gospel directly from the Lord' (G. E. Ladd, 'Revelation and Tradition in Paul': *Apostolic History and the Gospel*, p. 230).

*V*19: **But other of the apostles saw I none, save James the Lord's brother.**

The only other apostle whom Paul met on his first visit to Jerusalem after his conversion was James the Lord's brother. Although James was not a believer during the public ministry [*John* 7.5], a particular appearance of the Risen Lord was the means of his conversion [1 *Cor* 15.7], and he was now one of the 'pillars' [2.9] of the church in Jerusalem. The only sensible explanation of the word 'brother' is that this James was the son of Mary by Joseph [*Matt* 1.25], and therefore the Lord's younger brother [cf *Mark* 6.3].

'Can we characterize it otherwise than as a contumacious setting up of an artificial tradition above the written Word, if we insist upon it that "brother" must mean, not brother, but either cousin or one who is no blood-relation at all; that "first-born" does not imply other children subsequently born; that the limit fixed to separation does not imply subsequent union?' (J. B. Mayor, *The Epistle of St James*, p. lv).

*V*20: **Now touching the things which I write unto you, behold, before God, I lie not.**

Such a solemn confirmation of the truthfulness of this account would not have been necessary unless the Galatians had been told a very different story. 'It would seem that a totally different account of his visits to Jerusalem after his conversion, and of the relation he sustained to the elder apostles, had been in use among the Judaists, to undermine his independent authority and neutralize his teaching' (Eadie).

*V*21: **Then I came into the regions of Syria and Cilicia.**

Paul did not spend the whole fortnight in conversation with Peter! He preached so boldly in the city that he again put his life in jeopardy [*Acts* 9.28, 29]. At this time the Lord appeared to Paul in a vision, and told him to leave Jerusalem for the Jews there would not receive his testimony, 'And he said unto me, Depart: for I will send thee forth far hence unto the Gentiles' [*Acts* 22.17-21]. It was therefore in accordance with this divine commission that Paul departed for regions far removed from the influence of the Jerusalem apostles [*Acts* 9.30, 11.25, 26]. 'The name of Syria is placed before Cilicia, though the ministry at Tarsus preceded that at Antioch: for the latter was by far the more important and prolonged ministry. A further reason for placing Syria first was the subordinate position of Cilicia: for Roman Cilicia was, like Judaea, only a district of the great province of Syria, separately administered by an imperial procurator at Tarsus' (Rendall).

*V*22: **And I was still unknown by face unto the churches of Judaea which were in Christ:**

Because of this swift departure for distant places Paul remained personally unknown to the churches in Judaea (as distinguished from the church in Jerusalem), though they had heard much of him [*v* 23]. The fact that Paul was at once called to labour elsewhere took away all semblance of dependence upon the Jerusalem apostles, for had he worked under their direction he would have become a well-known figure among the Christians of Judaea.

in Christ: This is what distinguishes the Christian church from the Jewish synagogue. Either a church *in* Christ or *no* church! Paul emphasizes the relationship which makes the church what it is: the body of Christ [*Eph* 1.22, 23].

*V*23: **but they only heard say, He that once persecuted us now preacheth the faith of which he once made havoc; 24 and they glorified God in me.**

Thus hearsay was Paul's only link with the Judaean Christians. Reports kept reaching them of how he who was once notorious for his persecution of believers was now famous for preaching the faith he had vainly attempted to suppress. 'It is a striking proof of the large space occupied by "faith" in the mind of the infant Church, that it should so soon have passed into a synonym for the Gospel. See *Acts* 6.7' (J. B. Lightfoot).

As they kept hearing reports of Paul's missionary work, so they kept on glorifying *God* (placed last for emphasis) as the evident Author of this amazing transformation *in* Paul.

When those who had only suffered from the attentions of a persecutor recognized the hand of God in his ministry, how could those who had only benefited from the labours of an apostle even begin to doubt it? Moreover, the acknowledgement that the faith Paul now preached was the same as their own showed that the pseudo-faith of the Judaizers was not the apostolic faith of the church.

CHAPTER TWO

On Paul's second visit to Jerusalem fourteen years later he was accompanied by Barnabas, and Titus, who, though a Greek, was not circumcised despite the pressure of the Judaizers. For Paul was determined to maintain the freedom of Gentile converts from the bondage of the law [vv 1–5]. As for the Jerusalem apostles they added nothing to Paul's ministry, and their recognition of his mission to the Gentiles clearly showed that they regarded him as an equal partner in the Lord's work [vv 6–10]. Paul gave further proof of his apostolic authority when he publicly rebuked Peter at Antioch for his inconsistent separation from the Gentiles [vv 11–14]. He took this stand because he saw that Jews who were saved by faith in Christ could not ask Gentiles to place any reliance on the law for their acceptance with God. Union with Christ means that Paul's obedience is secured through faith in the Son of God who loved him and gave himself for him. But to seek righteousness by the law is a denial of God's grace and makes Christ's death a thing of nought [vv 15B21].

V1: Then after the space of fourteen years I went up again to Jerusalem with Barnabas, taking Titus also with me.

When Paul was next in Jerusalem he had been an apostle for fourteen years. Two brief contacts in fourteen years hardly proved his alleged dependence upon the authority of the

Jerusalem church! As the second visit took place in AD 46, this would suggest AD 33 as the probable date of his conversion according to the ancient 'inclusive' system of reckoning. 'The grand moment of his life was his conversion, and it became the point from which dates were unconsciously measured – all before it fading away as old and legal, all after it standing out in new and spiritual prominence . . . Had this verse occurred immediately after 1.18, we might have said that the fourteen years dated from the first visit to Jerusalem; but a paragraph intervenes which obscures the reference, and describes some time spent and some journeys made in various places, It is natural, therefore, to suppose, that after a digressive insertion, the apostle recurs to the original point of calculation – his conversion' (Eadie).

I went up again to Jerusalem with Barnabas, This must refer to the projected 'famine relief visit' of *Acts* 11.29f and its later accomplishment, *Acts* 12.25. Calvin saw clearly that it could not be identified with the visit to attend the Council of Jerusalem recorded in *Acts* 15, and therefore judged that the Epistle was written before it was held. For he said, Paul 'would never have alluded to that journey, undertaken with the consent of all believers, without mentioning its occasion and its memorable outcome'. Barnabas had been sent by the Jerusalem church to investigate the thriving work among the Gentiles at Syrian Antioch. On seeing much evidence of the grace of God in their midst, he determined to seek the assistance of Paul whom he brought from Tarsus. Their first opportunity to report on the progress of the Gentile mission came when they were entrusted to bring this gift from the 'Christians' of Antioch [*Acts* 11.19–30].

taking Titus also with me. The presence of Titus was to give rise to a debate, the importance of which was out of all proportion to his subordinate position in the party. For he was a Gentile, and perhaps Paul took him along to see whether brotherly love for a fellow-believer would triumph over Jewish prejudice.

V2: **And I went up by revelation; and I laid before them the gospel which I preach among the Gentiles but privately before them who were of repute, lest by any means I should be running, or had run, in vain.**

(It was in consequence of a revelation that I went up at all.) (Moffatt) As it took a vision to make Paul leave Jerusalem [*Acts* 22.21], so it required a similar revelation from the Lord to induce him to return. He was no stranger to such revelations, for the Lord who called him, also constantly guided him in the way he should go. Perhaps this was made known to him through the prophecy of Agabus [*Acts* 11.28], though a direct revelation seems more probable. What Paul wants the Galatians to know is that it was not with any feeling of dependence that he went up to this earthly seat of power and influence, for the source of his authority, no less than that of the other apostles, was Jerusalem above.

and I set before them the gospel which I preach among the Gentiles – privately, I mean, to the 'men of repute' among them, (Bruce) Compare also NEB. Although other business had brought Paul to Jerusalem, he welcomed the opportunity privately to acquaint the leaders of the church with the exact nature of the message he had always preached, and still did preach among the Gentiles. It is not likely that Paul would have submitted his gospel for the approval of the *members* of the Jerusalem church, though it was necessary to secure the sanction of its *leaders*; not to validate his message, but to avoid the tragedy of a split between the Gentile and

Jewish wings of the church. In itself there is nothing ironical in the term 'men of repute', but its repeated use in this passage [*v* 6] suggests an awareness of the exaggerated esteem in which these men were held by the Judaizers, who had probably told the Galatians that Paul was not one of the 'pillar' apostles [*v* 9].

lest by any means I should be running, or had run, in vain. The stadium foot race is one of Paul's favourite metaphors when speaking of his apostolic calling [*1 Cor* 9.24, 26; *Phil* 2.16; *2 Tim* 4.7]. He feared that his strenuous missionary efforts would be in vain if the authorities in Jerusalem failed to endorse the 'free' gospel the Gentiles had received from him. For to insist upon Gentile compliance with the demands of the ceremonial law would in effect introduce them to 'another' gospel [1.7].

*V*3 : **But not even Titus who was with me, being a Greek, was compelled to be circumcised: 4 and that because of the false brethren privily brought in, who came in privily to spy out our liberty which we have in Christ Jesus, that they might bring us into bondage: 5 to whom we gave place in the way of subjection, no, not for an hour; that the truth of the gospel might continue with you.**

But even Titus, who was with me, was not compelled to be circumcised, though he was a Greek. (RSV) It was not to be expected that Paul's choice of an uncircumcised Greek for his companion would meet with universal approval in Jerusalem. Thus the presence of Titus constituted a testcase, and the fact that he was not compelled to be circumcised, though this was strongly pressed by the Judaizers, really amounted to a declaration of principle. 'The apostle is showing that he had not laboured in vain, – that the very point which characterized his gospel was gained, that point being the free admission of uncircumcised Gentiles into the church; for even in Jerusalem the circumcision of Titus was successfully resisted, – the enemy was worsted even in his citadel' (Eadie).

But because of false brethren (RSV) Paul's meaning is plain enough, though the connection is broken under the stress of emotion. The Jerusalem apostles are not the culprits who caused this controversy, but certain false brethren ('sham-Christians' NEB) whose representations may well have caused these 'pillars' to waver, not realizing that a vital principle was at stake. As Lightfoot says, this view of the matter is 'consistent with the timid conduct of Peter at Antioch shortly after [2.11], and with the politic advice of James at a later date [*Acts* 21.20]. It was the natural consequence of their position, which led them to regard tenderly the scruples of the Jewish converts.'

secretly brought in, who slipped in to spy out (RSV) 'The metaphor is that of spies or traitors introducing themselves by stealth into the enemy's camp ... The camp thus stealthily entered is the Christian Church. Pharisees at heart, these traitors assume the name and garb of believers' (Lightfoot).

our freedom which we have in Christ Jesus, (RSV) Not merely freedom from the Mosaic ritual, but included within it justification by faith without the deeds of the law. 'Its element of being is "in Christ Jesus", not by Him though He did secure it, but in Him through living faith, and in Him by fellowship with Him. By Him it was secured to us, but in Him we possess it' (Eadie).

that they might bring us into bondage – (RSV) It was the intention of the Judaizers to bring all Gentile converts under the yoke of the law, but it was Paul alone who saw that the adoption of this error would reduce Christ's 'free men' to a condition of abject slavery [5.1].

to them we did not yield submission even for a moment, that the truth of the gospel might be preserved for you. (RSV) Paul did not pause to deliberate the issue. His resistance to this demand was immediate and unyielding. He would not sacrifice 'the truth of the gospel' – the *truth* which is the gospel's distinctive element – simply to soothe the ruffled feelings of *false* brethren! Thus Titus the Greek was not circumcised so that the gospel might be preserved in its integrity for the Gentiles, including the Galatians ('you').

*V*6: **But from those who were reputed to be somewhat (whatsoever they were, it maketh no matter to me: God accepteth not man's person) – they, I say, who were of repute imparted nothing to me:**

And from those who were reputed to be something (RSV) Having dealt with the question of Titus, Paul takes up the thread of verse 2. But now the 'men of repute' have become 'those who are looked up to as authorities', a description that 'is depreciatory, not indeed of the Twelve themselves, but of the extravagant and exclusive claims set up for them by the Judaizers' (Lightfoot).

(what they once were, it maketh no matter to me: God accepteth not man's person) (ASV margin) The fact that these men had known Jesus 'after the flesh' [2 *Cor* 5.16] made no difference to Paul, though it meant everything to his opponents, who were wholly preoccupied with an external glorying in the flesh [cf 6.13]. 'Paul simply means that the noble position which the apostles held did not prevent his having been called by God and raised suddenly from being nothing to becoming their equal. Although the difference between them had been great, it was nothing in God's sight, for He does not accept persons and His calling is not influenced by any prejudice' (Calvin).

– those, I say, who were of repute added nothing to me; (RSV) 'that is to say, they neither modified his teaching nor added to his authority' (W. E. Vine). When Paul laid before these 'authorities' the gospel he preached among the Gentiles, they accepted it without amendment or addition. This meant that in requiring the Galatians to submit to circumcision, the Judaizers were seeking to enforce what the Jerusalem apostles had never enjoined.

*V*7: **but contrariwise, when they saw that I had been intrusted with the gospel of the uncircumcision, even as Peter with** *the gospel* **of the circumcision**

but on the contrary when they saw that I had been entrusted with the gospel to the uncircumcised as Peter with the gospel to the circumcised (Burton) But far from condemning Paul's practice, the Jerusalem apostles endorsed it for they perceived that God had entrusted him with the task of taking the gospel to the Gentiles, even as Peter's sphere was to preach it to the Jews, though this was not a hard and fast division of labour [e.g. *Acts* 10.34ff; 13.16ff]. Jew and Gentile both received the *same* gospel, but 'circumcision formed the point of difference. The Jew might practise it, for it was a national rite; but it was not to be enforced on the Gentile' (Eadie).

*V*8: **(for he that wrought for Peter unto the apostleship of the circumcision wrought for me also unto the Gentiles);**

For it was evident that the same God who worked by Peter in his mission to the Jews also worked by Paul in his mission to the Gentiles. In each case the manifestation of divine power was the incontrovertible proof of a divine commission. In thus reminding his converts of the effectiveness of his ministry, Paul tacitly rebukes them for their disloyalty in listening to the false claims of the Judaizers.

V9: **and when they perceived the grace that was given to me, James and Cephas and John, they who were reputed to be pillars, gave to me and Barnabas the right hands of fellowship, that we should go unto the Gentiles, and they unto the circumcision;**

and when they perceived the grace that was given to me, At this momentous private meeting [v 2] Paul's stirring exposition of his gospel evidently made a powerful impression upon these 'pillars' of the Jerusalem church. 'They came to a knowledge of the divine gift enjoyed by Paul, implying that they had not distinctly understood it before. If they added nothing to Paul [v 6], he certainly added something to them' (Eadie). The undeserved favour of God to which Paul owed his commission is here underlined by his use of the word 'grace' [cf Eph 3.8]

James and Cephas and John, they who were reputed to be pillars, It is in accord with the important part that James [1.19] was later to play in the Council of Jerusalem that his name is placed first [Acts 15]. For while Peter was the leader in missionary work among the Jews, James seems to have early attained a position of great influence in the church at Jerusalem. As in the early chapters of Acts, John (mentioned only here in Paul's Epistle) again appears as Peter's associate. Paul recognizes these men to be *pillars* 'being such as God made use of in the first founding and building of the gospel church; as also to bear it up', but qualifies this by the word *reputed* 'because the false teachers had magnified their ministry, but disparaged his' (Matthew Poole).

gave to me and Barnabas the right hands of fellowship, In a day when it is deemed expedient to suppress the truth in the interests of church unity, it is worth noting with J. G. Machen that it is only by having the gospel in common that there is any basis for fellowship at all. In extending the right hands of fellowship to Paul and Barnabas, the Jerusalem leaders acknowledged that they were serving the same Lord, and preaching the same gospel. Such mutual 'fellowship' in the gospel was indeed a far cry from the 'inferior' position assigned to Paul by the Judaizers!

that we should go unto the Gentiles, and they unto the circumcision; 'The so-called "division of labour" between Paul and the original apostles was not, strictly speaking, a division of labour at all; its purpose was not negative; it was not meant at all as a limitation of the field of one party or of the other; it did not mean that Paul was not to preach to Jews or that Peter was not to preach to Gentiles; it did not mean that Paul was not to preach in Palestine or that Peter was not to preach outside of Palestine. But it meant that so far, according to the plain meaning of God, Paul had been sent predominantly to the Gentiles and the original apostles to the Jews; and that, therefore, unless both Paul and the original apostles continued their work, the cause would suffer' (Machen).

V10: **only** *they would* **that we should remember the poor; which very thing I was also zealous to do.**

'Only,' they said, 'please go on remembering the poor'; and in fact I had made a special point of attending to this

very matter. (Bruce) The only request made by these 'authorities' was that Paul and Barnabas should go on remembering the needs of the poor, which was the very thing that had brought them up to Jerusalem! [*Acts* 11.29ff; 12.25] Although Gentile believers were generally poor, they were relatively better off than their Jewish brethren, whose economic distress was made worse by religious discrimination. Paul uses the singular pronoun 'I' because the point at issue in Galatia turned on what the Jerusalem apostles had said to *him*, while the past tense ('had made') points back to the decision to send this aid, 'for though it was during the Jerusalem visit that the relief-work came to visible manifestation, the instigation of it lay in the past in Antioch' (Duncan).

*V*11: **But when Cephas came to Antioch, I resisted him to the face, because he stood condemned.**

When Paul later returned to Antioch after the first missionary journey, he had to rebuke Peter publicly for the inconsistency of his conduct in hiding his real convictions [*Acts* 10.28], by which 'he stood quite self-condemned' (Bruce). 'In this debated matter of Gentile freedom, while others stumbled or advanced with unsteady step . . . Paul moved onwards without hesitation or pause, and by his single courage and consistency secured to the churches a liberty which, though it might be grudged or suspected in many quarters, could not be withdrawn, but has descended as an invaluable legacy to modern times. As he knew Peter's character, it must have cost him a pang to confront him whose name stands first in all the catalogues of the apostles; but the claims of truth were paramount' (Eadie).

*V*12: **For before that certain came from James, he ate with the Gentiles; but when they came, he drew back**

and separated himself, fearing them that were of the circumcision.

For before certain individuals from James arrived he had been in the habit of eating his meals with the Gentiles. (W. Hendriksen) The arrival of envoys from James made Peter have second thoughts about the wisdom of openly fraternizing with the Gentile believers in Antioch. It seems that news of this had reached Jerusalem and was causing a grave scandal, especially since it had become known to un-believing Jews in the city. James therefore appealed to Peter to desist from this practice to save further embarrassment to the church in Jerusalem.[1] However, these men doubtless exceeded their brief when they insisted upon circumcision as a condition of salvation [*Acts* 15.1], for James would not have gone back on his earlier agreement with Paul [2.9].

But when they came he gradually drew back and separated himself, (Burton) The tenses 'give a graphic picture of Peter's irresolute and tentative efforts to withdraw gradually from an intercourse that gave offence to the visitors' (Rendall). Under the influence of these representations Peter's loyalty to his convictions was worn away until he acted a part to save his reputation [*v* 12]. So easily did the apostle who opened the door of faith to the Gentiles [*Acts* 10.34ff] change like a chameleon into Peter the Pharisee, the separated one! 'The whole incident is remarkably characteristic of Peter – ever the first to recognize, and the first to draw back from, great principles and truths' (Henry Alford).

fearing the circumcision party. (RSV) So much for the stability of that 'Rock' upon which Rome claims to build! In once more falling a prey to moral cowardice [*Mark* 14.66ff],

1. So F. F. Bruce in *New Testament History*, p. 267.

Peter proved that 'the fear of man bringeth a snare' [*Prov* 29.25]. (Cf. his later stand for the truth: *Acts* 15.7ff.)

V13 : **And the rest of the Jews dissembled likewise with him; insomuch that even Barnabas was carried away with their dissimulation.**

And the rest of the Jews joined him in playing the hypocrite, so that even Barnabas was carried along by their hypocrisy. (Hendriksen) Such was the power of Peter's bad example that not only was it followed by the other Jewish believers in Antioch, but even Paul's trusted colleague, so recently returned from the first mission to the Gentiles, was swept away by the strong current of this hypocrisy. The word 'even' highlights the gravity of the crisis, and also shows how the unexpected defection of Barnabas must have cut Paul to the quick. This one lapse of Barnabas, who had been such a true 'son of encouragement' to Paul [*Acts* 9.27; 11.25f], demonstrates 'the danger of theological compromise, the besetting sin of loving natures' (R. A. Cole).

'If Peter and Barnabas had changed their views, hypocrisy could not have been laid to their charge. But with their opinions unchanged, they acted as if they had been changed; therefore are they accused of dissimulation ... This dissimulation, so wide and powerful, was compromising the freedom of the gospel, for it was subverting the doctrine of justification by faith; and therefore the apostle, who could on fitting occasions "to the Jews become a Jew", was obliged to visit it with immediate and stern rebuke' (Eadie).

V14 : **But when I saw that they walked not uprightly according to the truth of the gospel, I said unto Cephas before *them* all, If thou, being a Jew, livest as do the Gentiles, and not as do the Jews, how compellest thou the Gentiles to live as do the Jews?**

But when I saw that they were not pursuing a straight course in accordance with the truth of the gospel, (Hendriksen) Only Paul saw that Peter's conduct was such a contradiction of his convictions that it was bound to lead many astray. Although Peter's error was not doctrinal but practical, Paul perceived that its implications were harmful to the truth of the gospel, which they were both committed to uphold. Hence Paul did not hesitate to withstand even an apostle of such prestige as Peter.

I said unto Cephas before *them* all, 'This example teaches us that those who have sinned publicly must be chastised publicly, so far as it concerns the Church. The aim is that their sin may not, by remaining unpunished, do harm by its example. And elsewhere [1 *Tim* 5.20] Paul expressly says that this should be observed in regard to elders, because the office they hold makes their bad example more harmful' (Calvin).

'If you, though a Jew, live like a Gentile and not like a Jew, how can you compel the Gentiles to live like Jews?' (RSV) These are the actual words Paul used, while the following verses recall his general argument especially as it related to the contemporary situation in Galatia. If Peter, though born and bred a Jew, normally ignored Jewish food taboos and mixed freely with Gentiles, then it was quite unreasonable of him to *compel* the Gentiles to conform to these customs and live like Jews: 'i.e. practically oblige them, though such was not his intention. The force of his example, concealing his true principles, became a species of compulsion' (Lightfoot).

*V*15: **We being Jews by nature, and not sinners of the Gentiles, 16 yet knowing that a man is not justified by the works of the law but through faith in Jesus Christ, even we believed on Christ Jesus, that we might be justified by faith in Christ, and not by the works of the**

law: because by the works of the law shall no flesh be justified.

We ourselves, though by nature Jews and not 'Gentile sinners', (Hendriksen) The purpose of this concessive statement is to strengthen what follows: 'Though we are Jews by descent, and not Gentiles who as such are regarded by us from our elevation as sinners, yet our Judaism, with all its boasted superiority, could not bring us justification. Born and bred Jews as we are, we were obliged to renounce our trust in Judaism, for it was powerless to justify us. Why then go back to it, and be governed by it, as if we had not abandoned it at all?' (Eadie). In verse 16 Paul establishes this vital truth of the gospel in three propositions of increasing emphasis.

yet knowing that a man is not justified by the works of the law but through faith in Jesus Christ, The apostle first makes the general statement that *a man* (i.e. any man) is not justified by the works of law but only through faith in Jesus Christ. 'Yet knowing' shows that he is not revealing some new truth for the first time; he is reminding Peter of what they as apostles of Christ are both committed to uphold. As 'law' here lacks the article, some have thought that a wider reference is intended, but to the Jewish mind there was only one law, and that was the law which God had given them through his servant Moses. Paul's contribution to the doctrine of justification may be gauged from the fact that he is responsible for twenty-nine of the thirty-nine occurrences of the verb 'justify' in the New Testament. J. I. Packer also defines what justification means to Paul: it is *'God's act of remitting the sins of guilty men, and accounting them righteous, freely, by His grace, through faith in Christ, on the ground, not of their own works, but of the representative law-keeping and redemptive blood-shedding of the Lord Jesus Christ on their behalf'* ('Justification': *The New Bible Dictionary*, p. 682). Here the preposition 'through' points to faith as the sole *means* by which the sinner is enabled to lay hold of Christ and all his saving benefits.

even we believed on Christ Jesus, that we might be justified by faith in Christ, and not by the works of the law: The second statement sets forth what Paul and Peter both knew from personal experience. For despite our pedigree and privileges, we have committed ourselves to Christ for salvation, so that we might be justified 'out of' faith in him, and not 'out of' the works of the law. This change of preposition is probably intended to bring out the contrast between faith and works (so D. Guthrie). Consequently, 'even we' Jews who once thought we had righteousness by works of law, became just like the ignorant 'Gentile sinners' [*v* 15] who trusted in nothing but the doing and dying of Christ on their behalf.

because by the works of the law shall no flesh be justified. Finally, Paul quotes Scripture to show that the principle of non-justification by the works of the law is of universal application [*Ps* 143.2]. To achieve righteousness by the law is far beyond the power of frail flesh, because all men stand condemned by their inability to fulfil its comprehensive demands. Although the words 'by works of law' are not in the *Psalm*, there is 'a basis for them in the preceding line, "Enter not into judgment with thy servant", which gives to the words that Paul has quoted the sense, "no man can be justified if judged on a basis of merit, all grace and mercy on God's part being excluded"' (Burton).

*V*17: **But if, while we sought to be justified in Christ, we ourselves also were found sinners, is Christ a minister of sin? God forbid.**

Paul now asks: 'But if we Jews, in seeking to be justified in Christ apart from the works of the law, thus turn out to be no better than "Gentile sinners" [*v* 15], is Christ then a minister of sin?' Since we have renounced *law-keeping* as the ground of our justification, and thereby placed ourselves on the same level as Gentile *law-breakers*, are the Judaizers then right to conclude that this 'lawless' doctrine makes Christ a promoter of sin? Paul does not stop to argue the point, but at once repudiates the very suggestion that Christ could be regarded as the author of sin.

*V*18: **For if I build up again those things which I destroyed, I prove myself a transgressor.**

Paul tactfully uses the first person singular to set forth the consequences of Peter's inconsistency. Peter had torn down by his preaching and conduct the idea that works contributed to a man's justification, but his renewed submission to Jewish dietary laws was virtually a building up again of that erroneous opinion. For in yielding to the demands of the Judaizers, Peter had given occasion for others to suppose that he looked upon such obedience to the law as an essential supplement to faith in Christ. His conduct thus belied his faith and fostered the impression that justification might be attained by an amalgam of grace and works. But God's holy law demands far more than the paltry, piecemeal 'fulfilment' that guilty sinners can bring to it! [*v* 21; 3.10] Since the very completeness of the divine code called for Christ as its perfect Fulfiller, 'reconstruction of the same materials is in respect of the law not only a tacit avowal of "sin" in having pulled it down, but is a real and definite "transgression" of all its deeper principles' (C. J. Ellicott). [*v* 19]

*V*19: **For I through the law died unto the law, that I might live unto God.**

For I through the law died unto the law, The emphatic 'I' shows that Paul is calling upon his own experience to explain the preceding assertion. Paul died to the law as a legal demand in the person of his Saviour who satisfied its claims and endured its curse on his behalf [*v* 20; 3.13]. 'As our Representative in whom we were chosen and in whom we suffered, He yielded Himself to the law, which seized Him and nailed Him to the cross. When that law seized Him, it seized at the same time all his in Him, and through the law they suffered and died to it ... And now certainly, if the law, avenging itself on our guilt, has in this way wrought our release from itself – has set us for ever free from its yoke, and we have died to it and have done with it; then he who would re-enact legalism and bring men under it, proves himself its transgressor, nay, opposes its deepest principles and its most gracious design' (Eadie). [*Rom* 6.6-13; 7.1-6]

that I might live unto God. But freedom from the law is not lawlessness. The supreme purpose for which Christ confers life and liberty is that those thus redeemed may no longer live unto themselves but unto God. And this dedication to God is expressed by their delight in his law as *their rule of duty*. For though Paul had died to the condemning power of the law, he did not see himself as being 'without law to God, but under law to Christ' [1 *Cor* 9.21]. Now believers are free from the law in four respects. 'First, in respect of the accusing, and damnatory sentence of the law, *Rom* 8.1. Secondly, in respect of the power of the law, whereby as an occasion it provoketh and stirreth up the corruption of the heart in the unregenerate, *Rom* 7.8. Thirdly, in respect of the rigour of the law, whereby it exacteth most perfect obedience for our justification. Thus *Paul* here saith, that *he is dead to the law*. Lastly, in respect of the obligation of the conscience, to the observation of ceremonies, *Col* 2.20. Thus are all persons justified by the faith of Christ, free from the law' (Perkins).

*V*20: **I have been crucified with Christ; and it is no longer I that live, but Christ liveth in me: and that *life* which I now live in the flesh I live in faith, *the faith* which is in the Son of God, who loved me, and gave himself up for me.**

With Christ I have been crucified; This explains the previous verse and shows how Paul died to the law. 'Paul uses the perfect tense in speaking of his having died with Christ, that is, in speaking of something that once took place and has not lost its power since. This thing that has happened somewhere else in the past does not refer to Paul's subjective experience, but to the death of Christ. The believers, by virtue of their corporate belonging to Him, were included in that dying' (Ridderbos).

and it is no longer I that live, but Christ liveth in me: Paul's meaning is not that his own personality has ceased to exist, but that it is so transformed by Christ's living in him that he no longer recognizes his former sinful self (*John* 15.4, 5). Having experienced so great a deliverance from legalism, Paul could never travel that road again. But the Galatians, who are on the brink of such a fatal relapse, must learn that submission to a régime of law would sever their union with the Christ who was the sole source of their spiritual life [*Col* 3.4].

and that *life* which I now live in the flesh I live in faith, *the faith* which is in the Son of God, Faith is the secret of Paul's new life, and it is a faith which rests on the Son of God himself. '*Faith*, not the *flesh*, is the real element in which I live. The phrase, "the Son of God", reminds us that his divine Sonship is the source of his life-giving power' (A. R. Fausset). It is therefore because the Christian life is a life of faith in the Son of God that it excludes all reliance upon oneself or one's works.

who loved me, and gave himself up for me. Paul's whole life is dominated by the thought that the Son of God so loved him that He willingly gave Himself up to death for him (i.e. in his stead). Such personal pronouns express the very essence of saving faith. 'No matter who else were loved, He loved me; no matter for whom other He gave Himself, He gave Himself for me. Is it any wonder, then, that my life even now is a life of faith in Him, and no longer one in legal bondage? . . . He must deny himself and forget all his previous history, before he could turn his back on that cross where the Son of God proved the intensity and self-denying nature of His love for him in that atonement which needs neither repetition nor supplement. "Wilt thou bring thy cowl, thy shaven crown, thy chastity, thy obedience, thy poverty, thy works, thy merits? What shall these do?" (Luther)' (Eadie).

*V*21: **I do not make void the grace of God: for if right-eousness is through the law, then Christ died for nought.**

The apostle's concluding statement is a ringing affirmation of his determination to uphold the grace of God in the face of all temporizing expedients. It is, as Machen rightly says, the key verse of the Epistle and expresses its central thought. It was because Paul refused to make void God's grace that he did not stand by in silence when the truth of the gospel was compromised by Peter's dissimulation [*v* 11]. For he realized that if righteousness could be attained through the law, then Christ died in vain. If his sacrifice did not secure our *complete* salvation, then he died to no purpose! 'The Judaizers attempted to supplement the saving work of Christ by the merit of their own obedience to the law. "That", says Paul, "is impossible; Christ will do everything or nothing: earn your salvation if your obedience to the law is perfect, or else trust wholly to Christ's completed work; you cannot do both; you cannot combine merit and grace; if justification even in the slightest measure is through human merit, then Christ died in vain"' (Machen).

CHAPTER THREE

*Having refuted the claims of the Judaizers from personal experience
[1.10–2.21], Paul next shows that such reliance on the deeds of the
law is not in accord with the testimony of Scripture [3.1–4.31].
Since the Galatians had become Christians by believing the gospel,
it would be the height of folly if they now reverted to the law, and
exchanged the blessings of the Spirit for the works of the flesh
[vv 1–5]. For as Abraham was justified by faith, so his blessing
belongs to those who share his faith [vv 6–9]. The law could do
no more than bring all men under its curse, from which we were
redeemed by Christ who took our curse upon himself, so that we
might receive the promised blessing through faith [vv 10–14]. And
as even the covenants of men cannot be modified, it is evident that
God's promise to Abraham has an abiding validity which could not
be made void by the later provisions of the law [vv 15–18]. This
does not mean that the law has no function, for its purpose was to
prepare the way for Christ. The law shuts up all under sin, and
thus acted as our tutor to bring us to Christ. But now that faith has
delivered us from its strict supervision, we are all sons of God and
Abraham's true spiritual heirs, for in Christ all human distinctions
have ceased to count [vv 19–29].*

V1: **O foolish Galatians, who did bewitch you, before
whose eyes Jesus Christ was openly set forth crucified?**

**O senseless Galatians, who has bewitched you – you who
had Jesus Christ the crucified placarded before your**

very eyes? (Moffatt) Paul's passionate remonstrance is an appeal to the Galatians' spiritual experience. Their senseless folly in giving credence to the perverted gospel of the Judaizers showed such 'an unworthy lack of understanding' (Vine), that to speak figuratively, they seemed like those hypnotized by some malign spell. For what else could explain their removing from the gospel of 'Christ crucified' [1 Cor 1.23; 2.2] when this truth has been placarded so plainly before them in Paul's preaching? The reference is to spiritual perception and not of course to any visual representation of Christ [cf v 2: 'the *hearing* of faith'). 'This is the indictment against the Galatians: all this placarding was so plain to the eye, and yet they acted as though they could not see, had no sense to read, could not think what this meant. "Crucified – crucified – crucified!" – even a little thinking should suffice to turn the Galatians against all Judaizers. The entire Scriptures are so placarded, yet men even preach on them and see nothing in the cross except noble martyrdom [2 Cor 4.3, 4]' (R. C. H. Lenski).

*V*2: **This only would I learn from you, Received ye the Spirit by the works of the law, or by the hearing of faith?**

The Galatians could return but one answer to this question. They had received the Spirit not by obeying the law but by believing the gospel. It was through the hearing of faith that they came to know that Spirit without whom no man can say 'Jesus is Lord' [1 Cor 12.3] – 'that Spirit which enlightens, sanctifies, certifies of sonship, makes intercession for us as being in us, seals us, and is the earnest and first-fruits' (Eadie). However, they were now being mesmerized by the 'Higher Life' teaching of the Judaizers which promised far greater blessings than these, if only they would fully yield themselves to God by obeying the demands of his holy law! But since the reception of the Spirit is nothing less than a receiving of Christ in all the fulness of his saving grace, only those who fail to see the greatness of the initial bestowment can be deceived by the teaching that God's free grace can be *supplemented* by our obedience. 'So the error of the Judaizers is a very modern error indeed, as well as a very ancient error. It is found in the modern Church wherever men seek salvation by "surrender" instead of by faith, or by their own character instead of by the imputed righteousness of Christ, or by "making Christ master in the life" instead of by trusting in His redeeming blood' (Machen).

*V*3: **Are ye so foolish? having begun in the Spirit, are ye now perfected in the flesh?**

Are ye so foolish? having begun in the Spirit, do ye now make an end in the flesh? (ASV margin) This is really one question which reveals the extent of the Galatians' folly by pointing a double contrast. Their good beginning in the faith is contrasted with the tragic completion proposed by the Judaizers, and the life-giving power of the Spirit is contrasted with the futility of ending with the flesh. 'They are insane men who do not understand what the Spirit or the flesh is. The Spirit is whatever is done in us through the Spirit; the flesh is whatever is done in us in accordance with the flesh and apart from the Spirit ... By "flesh" he does not mean sexual lust, animal passions, or the sensual appetite, because in this passage he is not discussing sexual lust or other desires of the flesh. No, he is discussing the forgiveness of sins, the justification of the conscience, the attainment of righteousness in the sight of God, and liberation from the Law, sin, and death. And yet he says here that after they have forsaken the Spirit, they are now being ended with the flesh. Thus "flesh" is the very righteousness and wisdom of the flesh and the judgment of reason, which wants to be justified through the

Law. Therefore whatever is best and most outstanding in man Paul calls "flesh", namely, the highest wisdom of reason and the very righteousness of the Law' (Luther).

V4: **Did ye suffer so many things in vain? if it be indeed in vain.**

Have you had such remarkable experiences in vain? (Arndt-Gingrich) This translation is preferable as the idea of suffering or persecution is quite foreign to the context. Paul asks whether they will contradict their experience of that more abundant life which Christ had brought to them by his Spirit? Having experienced Christian freedom, will they now be guilty of relapsing into Jewish legalism?

if it be indeed in vain. This is added because Paul cannot bring himself to believe that their good beginning in the faith was after all to no purpose. Thus he shows them that he still hopes that his appeal will lead to their amendment.

V5: **He therefore that supplieth to you the Spirit, and worketh miracles among you, *doeth he it* by the works of the law, or by the hearing of faith?**

In verse 2 Paul reminds the Galatians of their reception of the Spirit; here he directs their attention to God as the Giver of the Spirit. He uses the present tense not specially to refer to their present experience of the Spirit, but to characterize God as the Supplier of the Spirit. Thus Eadie explains: 'God, whose prerogative it is to give the Spirit and work miracles, – does He, is He in the habit of giving the one and doing the other by the works of the law or by the hearing of faith?' It was impossible for the Galatians to evade the force of this question. They knew from personal experience that the law-message of the Judaizers was powerless to impart the spiritual graces and gifts they had received by believing the message of faith! Paul's insistence upon the 'hearing of faith' as the *exclusive* means through which God bestows the Spirit therefore leads to the inescapable conclusion that they would forfeit their great spiritual privileges by declining to the 'works of the law' (F. D. Bruner).

*V*6: **Even as Abraham believed God, and it was reckoned unto him for righteousness.**

This appeal to the Galatians' experience [*vv* 1–5] is now confirmed by the testimony of Scripture [*Gen* 15.6]. As Paul's doctrinal argument is largely centred upon the example of Abraham [*vv* 6, 7, 8, 9, 14, 16, 18, 29; 4.22], it seems reasonable to assume that he is refuting the false conclusions which the Judaizers had drawn from the patriarch's life (see comment on *v* 7). But Paul quotes this verse to show that Abraham's acceptance with God was found through believing the divine promise [*Gen* 15.5], for his faith was 'reckoned' or credited to him for righteousness.

This means that 'the non-righteous Abraham stood before the divine tribunal acquitted and accepted as truly as if he had possessed a personal righteousness through uniform obedience. His faith, not as an act, but as a fact, put him into this position by God's own deed, without legal fiction or abatement ... He was lifted into acceptance with God, however, not on account of his faith, but through it laying hold of the promise. That faith had no merit; for what merit can a creature have in believing the Creator's word? – it is only bare duty, – but Abraham's trust in God introduced him into the promised blessing. His faith rested on the promise, and through that faith he became its possessor or participant. That promise, seen in the light of a previous utterance, included the Messiah; and with all which it contained, and with this as its central and pre-eminent object, it was laid hold of by his faith, so that his condition was tantamount to justification by faith in the righteousness of Christ' (Eadie). [cf. *Gen* 12.3; *John* 8.56]

*V*7: **Know therefore that they that are of faith, the same are sons of Abraham.**

This begins the apostle's answer to the argument of the Judaizers, who evidently taught that Gentiles who wished to be blessed with Abraham must receive the covenant-sign by which their participation in covenant-blessing would be assured [*Gen* 17.1–14]. But the mere reception of an external sign does not automatically confer internal grace [cf 6.15]. Paul's use of the imperative 'Know ye' shows that he is determined to teach the Galatians the lesson of *Gen* 15.6 [*v* 6] – a verse the Judaizers doubtless omitted to quote! For as Abraham's faith, which antedated his circumcision by many years, was the vital factor in his acceptance with God, so the possession of the same justifying faith is ever that which distinguishes his true 'sons' from those whose connection with him is purely physical [*Matt* 3.9; *John* 8.39; *Rom* 2.28, 29]. 'Not those who are descended from Abraham by ordinary generation, not those who have united themselves to Abraham's descendants by circumcision and the keeping of the law of Moses, certainly not those who have tried – vainly – to attain merit with God by any kind of observance of God's law, but those who have the same faith as that which Abraham had are his true sons and the true heirs of the promises which God gave to him' (Machen).

*V*8: **And the scripture, foreseeing that God would justify the Gentiles by faith, preached the gospel before-hand unto Abraham, *saying*, In thee shall all the nations be blessed.**

Paul now passes to another aspect of the same truth. It is no novelty that the Gentiles are saved by faith, for this was revealed to Abraham. 'It was not, however, the Scripture (which did not exist at the time) that, foreseeing God's purposes of grace in the future, spoke these precious words to Abraham, but God himself in his own person'. The apostle therefore could only attribute such an act to Scripture because he habitually regarded it 'as the living voice of God' (B. B. Warfield, *The Inspiration and Authority of the Bible*, pp. 299, 345). [cf *Rom* 9.17] Here the present tense, which underlies 'would justify', points to God's method of justifying by faith as the unchanging principle of the divine government.

Paul can say that God's first promise to Abraham was a prior preaching of the gospel [*Gen* 12.3], because it showed that the pattern of future blessing for the world would be found in connection with 'believing Abraham' [*v* 9]. Hence the nature of the Gentiles' union with Abraham ('in thee') was not what the Judaizers had supposed, for they were joined to him by faith and not by circumcision! So God, foreseeing his 'own gracious and uniform process of justifying the Gentile races through faith, made it known to Abraham, even while disclosing to him the blessing of his own promised and direct posterity. God revealed it, not to some heathen prince or priest, one of the Gentiles himself, but to the father of the Jewish race' (Eadie).

*V*9: **So then they that are of faith are blessed with the faithful Abraham.**

So that the men of faith are blessed with the faithful (believing) Abraham. (Burton) Thus only those who are also characterized by faith enjoy community of blessing with believing Abraham. The present tense shows that Gentile believers are not only given the prospect of future bliss, but are blessed by God – declared righteous – the moment they trust Christ for salvation. Since in both dispensations, the old

[59]

and the new, the one Saviour has but one people, the summit of blessing is found in company with faithful Abraham!

*V*10: **For as many as are of the works of the law are under a curse: for it is written, Cursed is every one who continueth not in all things that are written in the book of the law, to do them.**

Having established the truth of justification by faith from Scripture, Paul now confronts his bemused readers with three more texts which exhibit the folly of replacing the principle of faith with reliance upon the works of the law [*vv* 10–12]. Submission to the demands of the legalizers, far from bringing the Galatians the promised blessing, would actually place them under a curse, since all who break God's law are justly exposed to God's wrath. This means that if they remove from the blessings of faith, then they must incur the curse of the law. For to merit salvation by personal obedience is not an option that is open to violators of the law. Therefore sinners who wish to find acceptance with God must sue for grace and seek an interest in the justifying righteousness of Christ. The Scripture cited confirms that the law can bring only a curse to those unable to render exact and unvarying obedience to all its commands [*Deut* 27.26].

It is important to realize that the Judaizers divorced the law from the context of grace in which it had been given to Israel, for under the old economy the law remained subservient to the promise [3.17]. Consequently Israel's assent to all the curses pronounced on Mount Ebal is inexplicable apart from the promised Redeemer who was to be born 'under the law' [4.5], in order that he might exhaust its curse on their behalf [3.13]. And the fact that Christ would come to bear that curse for them 'was daily demonstrated to them by their sacrifices' (Herman Hoeksema, *Reformed Dogmatics*, p. 404).

*V*11: **Now that no man is justified by the law before God, is evident: for, The righteous shall live by faith;**

Having shown that salvation by law-keeping is impossible because man is disabled by sin, Paul goes on to prove from Scripture that in fact justification has never been by works but always by faith. And since it is God who established this connection between faith and salvation, it is evident that those who rely on the works of the law have no hope of securing a favourable verdict before the divine tribunal.

The righteous shall live by faith; Although the original Hebrew word is more accurately rendered as 'faithfulness', such fidelity in the face of mortal danger is only made possible by faith in the promises of God. So Paul is not guilty of distorting the prophet's message when he sees this faith as the *abiding principle* in the life of the righteous man. 'In *Habakkuk* 2.4 this faith is not set in contrast to the works of the law, however, but over against the arrogance and self-confidence of the wicked. Positively seen, though, the faith intended in *Hab* 2 and *Gal* 3 is essentially the same. It is a resting in God without regard to human care and effort' (Ridderbos). [cf *Rom* 1.17; *Heb* 10.38]

*V*12: **and the law is not of faith; but, He that doeth them shall live in them.**

and the law is not of faith; It is because the apostle knows that 'the law' and 'faith' are mutually exclusive principles that he challenges the 'both/and' of the false gospel with the 'either/or' of God's word. For to seek justification by obedience to the law is to renounce any interest in Christ's free salvation. The real point at issue between Paul and the Judaizers is well summarized by Machen. 'Paul said that a man (1) first believes on Christ, (2) then is justified before God, (3) then immediately proceeds to keep God's law. The Judaizers said that a man (1) believes on Christ and (2) keeps the law of God the best he can, and then (3) is justified.' The difference was not simply a matter of hair-splitting distinctions. It 'was the difference between two entirely distinct types of religion; it was the difference between a religion of merit and a religion of grace. If Christ provides only a part of our salvation, leaving us to provide the rest, then we are still hopeless under the load of sin' (Machen, *Christianity and Liberalism*, p. 24).

but, He that doeth them shall live in them. As with Paul's quotation of *Deut* 27.26 [*v* 10], when the principle set forth in *Lev* 18.5 was artificially isolated from its original setting in what was essentially a covenant of grace, it became a sentence of condemnation. Since Israel was merely the recipient of God's undeserved favour, their obedience to the law could not earn the blessings they already enjoyed. And though the retention of the inheritance was suspended upon Israel's obedience, it would be a mistake to interpret this condition in any legalistic sense. It rather typically represents the truth that the reception of grace must always be recorded in the register of gratitude. 'But the Judaizers went wrong in inferring that the connection must be *meritorious*, that, if Israel keeps the cherished gifts of Jehovah through observance of his law, this must be so, because in strict justice they had *earned* them' (Geerhardus Vos, *Biblical Theology*, p. 143). Thus Paul's polemic is directed against the legalism which demanded obedience to the law as a *condition* of salvation [cf *Acts* 15.24].

*V*13: **Christ redeemed us from the curse of the law, having become a curse for us; for it is written, Cursed is every one that hangeth on a tree:**

Christ The absence of any connecting particle is significant. 'Coming after all that has been said about the curse, the abrupt introduction of the name of Christ suggests the appearance on the scene of one who alone can deal with so tragic a situation' (Duncan).

redeemed us The word 'redeemed' focusses attention upon the cost of the deliverance wrought by Christ. He paid the price to set men free from the bondage of sin. This was no mere token payment, but a full satisfaction of the claims of divine justice. It was only because Christ was not in debt to the law himself that he could undertake to pay the debt of those who were under its condemning curse. Here the word 'us' can no more be restricted to Jews than the 'we' of the following verse limits the gift of the Spirit to Gentiles. This 'us' not only includes Paul and the Galatians, but also embraces all believers, whether Jews or Gentiles. For Gentiles, no less than Jews, needed to be ransomed from the curse of a broken law, though it was only written in their hearts [cf *Rom* 2.12–16].

from the curse of the law, having become a curse for us; The curse of the law means that every infraction of the law's demand must be visited with the wrath of God, so that in becoming the surety of a sinful people Christ was made in this official respect the object of divine wrath [*Matt* 27.46]. No words could more clearly express the penal and substitutionary nature of Christ's death. 'Without deliverance from this curse there could be no salvation. It is from this curse that Christ has purchased his people and the price of the purchase was that he himself became a curse. He became so identified with the curse resting upon his people that the whole of it in all its unrelieved intensity became his. That curse he bore and that curse he exhausted. That was the price paid for this redemption and the liberty secured for the beneficiaries is that there is no more curse' (John Murray, *Redemption Accomplished and Applied*, p. 44).

for it is written, Cursed is every one that hangeth on a tree: Crucifixion was not a Jewish punishment, and the quotation from *Deut* 21.23 originally referred to the hanging of the dead bodies of flagrant sinners on the tree of shame to show that they were accursed of God. 'So the very means of Christ's death showed it to be an accursed death. His being hanged on a tree proved that He was made a curse. The manner of the death, besides being in consonance with prophecy, was a visible proof and symbol of its real nature; for "He bore our sins in His own body on the tree". He bore the curse of a broken law, and the mode of His death signally showed that He became a curse, for, by being suspended on a stake, He became in the express terms of the law a curse. *Acts* 5.30, 10.39; I *Pet* 2.24' (Eadie).

*V*14: **that upon the Gentiles might come the blessing of Abraham in Christ Jesus; that we might receive the promise of the Spirit through faith.**

In two final clauses Paul states the gracious consequences of Christ's vicarious bearing of the curse. Both cover the same ground, the second establishing what is meant by the first.

that upon the Gentiles might come the blessing of Abraham in Christ Jesus; As Christ bore the curse to fulfil the promise made to Abraham that in him all nations would be blessed [*v* 9], so this blessing of Abraham comes upon the Gentiles only 'in Christ Jesus' – through the faith that comes to them [*vv* 23, 25], and not by their becoming 'Jews' [5.2]! Because Christ's death which brought deliverance from the curse also 'put an end to the typical and national economy from which the Gentiles were excluded, and introduced a

new dispensation without distinction of race or blood'
(Eadie). [*vv* 26-29; cf *Eph* 2.11-18]

**that we might receive the promise of the Spirit through
faith.** This harks back to verse 2. It is the comprehensive
boon of the promised Spirit received through faith *in conversion* that confers the blessing of Abraham in full measure
on both Jews and Gentiles. For it is the Spirit who puts men
'in Christ Jesus' and makes them sons of God by giving them
the saving faith that was in Abraham, whose trust in God's
Word made him the 'father' of all believers.

*V*15: **Brethren, I speak after the manner of men: Though
it be but a man's covenant, yet when it hath been confirmed, no one maketh it void, or addeth thereto.**

As Paul begins to explain the true relation of the law to the
promise, he appeals to his erring 'brethren' to follow his
argument, which he illustrates with 'an example from every-
day life' (NIV). He argues thus: even in human affairs when a
legal 'disposition' of property is once ratified, its provisions
cannot be set aside or modified in any way. This being so,
how much more does the same principle hold good with
God's sovereign 'disposition' of gospel grace, which has the
unconditional character of a one-sided grant. 'So legal
Judaism could make no alteration in the fundamental relation
between God and man, already established by the promises
to Abraham; it could not add as a new condition the observance of the law, in which case the fulfilment of the promise
would be attached to a condition impossible for man to
perform. The "covenant" here is one of free grace, a *promise*
afterwards carried into effect in the gospel' (Fausset).

*V*16: **Now to Abraham were the promises spoken, and
to his seed. He saith not, And to seeds, as of many;
but as of one, And to thy seed, which is Christ.**

[65]

Having shown the immutability of God's covenant, Paul now proceeds to identify those included within the scope of its oft-repeated promises. He insists that the true heirs of Abraham are not his natural descendants, for Christ is the 'seed' in whom alone these promises are fulfilled. This dictum has its objective basis in the distinction which God himself made between Ishmael and Isaac. For Abraham was told that 'in Isaac shall thy seed be called' [Gen 21.12; Rom 9.7; cf 4.28–31]. Moreover, it was later revealed to Isaac and Rebekah that the line of promise would be continued through Jacob and not Esau [Gen 25.23; Rom 9.8–13]. But if the promise did not embrace all the natural progeny of Abraham, it obviously could not be limited to the spiritual remnant of Israel, because it was centred upon Christ in whom all the nations were to be blessed. It therefore included all who would be brought to faith in Christ, whether Jews or Gentiles, for these alone are the true sons of believing Abraham [vv 26–29]. Thus the promised Messiah, 'the seed of the woman' [Gen 3.15], is the sum and substance of the promise, not as an individual, but as the Christ 'embodying at the same time His church – the Head with its members in organic unity' (Eadie).

*V*17: **Now this I say: A covenant confirmed beforehand by God, the law, which came four hundred and thirty years after, doth not disannul, so as to make the promise of none effect.**

This resumes the thought of verse 15. Paul's meaning is that what holds good for human covenants must apply in a pre-eminent degree to God's covenant. It is evident that the law which came so long after the promise cannot nullify the provisions of grace. But the Judaizers are placing the law above the promise, 'for they make obedience to the law the condition for obtaining the salvation granted by the promise'

(Ridderbos). A possible solution to the problems of chronology raised by this verse is put forward by E. J. Young, who suggests that the apostle's thought here is that the whole patriarchal period of the giving of the promise was separated from the period of the giving of the law by Israel's long sojourn of 430 years in the land of bondage (*Thy Word is Truth*, pp. 177–180). [cf *Exod* 12.40]

*V*18: **For if the inheritance is of the law, it is no more of promise: but God hath granted it to Abraham by promise.**

For if the inheritance is of the law, it is no more of promise: This unsound premise prepares the way for the irresistible conclusion which immediately follows it. If the inheritance is due to law, it clearly cannot be conferred by promise. Paul uses the same kind of argument in *Rom* 4.13f. His reasoning serves to show that the law and the promise are contradictory principles which cannot be combined, for 'that which is of grace, and of the promise, is of free love; that which is of works, and the law, is wages, and a reward of debt' (Poole).

but God hath granted it to Abraham by promise. But the fact of the matter is that God freely bestowed the inheritance on Abraham by way of promise. Here the perfect tense shows that the gift of God retains its character as the free grant of grace which remains in force for ever. Paul thus overthrows the false claims of the Judaizers by confronting the Galatians with this great historical fact which cannot be gainsaid. The covenant of grace that God established with Abraham could not be rescinded by the coming of the law, which was never intended to be the means of attaining the promised salvation. For what is earned by obedience cannot be received as a gift! 'The state of grace and favour with God here, and of glory hereafter, is the inheritance, portion, and heirship of the Lord's people, there being no temporal worldly inheritance which can sufficiently furnish the heart with satisfaction, *Ps* 4.6, 7, of which spiritual and heavenly inheritance the land of Canaan was a type; for the apostle, speaking of justification, and all the spiritual blessings which flow from it, calleth them the inheritance by way of excellency' (James Fergusson). [cf *Heb* 11.8 ff]

*V*19: **What then is the law? It was added because of transgressions, till the seed should come to whom the promise hath been made;** *and it was* **ordained through angels by the hand of a mediator.**

What then is the law? It was added because of transgressions, Paul here anticipates the inevitable objection, What then is the function of the law? His astonishing reply still further emphasizes the inferiority of the law to the promise. It was added alongside the promise, for the subordinate and temporary [*v* 23] purpose of bringing transgressions to light! 'For through the law cometh the knowledge of sin.' This axiom of the apostle's teaching was learned through the crucible of his own experience [cf *Rom* 3.20; 4.15; 5.20; 7.7, 13). Men 'may *sin* in ignorance, but they *transgress* only when they have a recognized standard of what is right, and it was to provide such a standard that the Law was brought in' (Duncan).

till the seed should come to whom the promise hath been made; The law was added in order to prepare for the coming of Christ 'by so deepening the sense of sinfulness that men, convicted of so often breaking it, could not look to it for righteousness, but must be "shut up unto the faith which should be afterwards revealed"' (Eadie).

and it was ordained by angels through an intermediary.
(RSV) Whereas the Jews gloried in the angelic mediation of
the law, Paul speaks of it in disparagement, because of the
distance it placed between God and men [cf *Deut* 33.2;
Ps 68.17; *Acts* 7.53; *Heb* 2.2]. 'The Promise was given directly
by God to Abraham; the Law was given indirectly, and
indeed doubly so, (*a*) by means of angels, (*b*) through Moses
... Luther expresses the thought of our passage when he
writes, "The Law is the voice of the servants, but the Gospel
is the voice of the Lord Himself"' (Williams). Thus the
Divine Mediator of the gospel cannot be compared with the
purely human intermediary through whom the law was
given.

*V*20: **Now a mediator is not *a mediator* of one; but God
is one.**

**Now an intermediary does not exist for one party
alone,** (Arndt-Gingrich) It is doubtless because the Judaizers
had laid great stress upon the importance of Moses that
Paul does not even mention him by name. Having said that
the law was given through an intermediary [*v* 19], the apostle
now tersely states that such an intermediary presupposes the
existence of at least two other parties between whom he is to
mediate. 'The Law then is of the nature of a contract between two parties, God on the one hand, and the Jewish
people on the other. It is only valid so long as both parties
fulfil the terms of the contract. It is therefore contingent and
not absolute' (Lightfoot).

but God is one. This emphasizes the unilateral character of
the covenant of grace. 'Unlike the law, the promise is absolute
and unconditional. It depends on the sole decree of God.
There are not two contracting parties. There is nothing of the

nature of a *stipulation*. The giver is everything, the recipient nothing' (Lightfoot).

V21: **Is the law then against the promises of God? God forbid: for if there had been a law given which could make alive, verily righteousness would have been of the law.**

In case it should seem that Paul is seeking to exalt the promise by depreciating the law, he boldly asks whether the law is contrary to God's promises, an inference which he at once repudiates with disgust. As the same God gave both the promise and the law it is evident that there can be no conflict between them. The law is itself holy for it makes known the will of a holy God, but it has no power to confer the righteousness it demands. Had there been given a law which could have imparted life to the spiritually dead, then righteousness would have been by the law. But the true function of the law, which only pronounces a curse upon the disobedient, is to drive sinners to trust in the promise [*v 22*]. 'The implication of the statement is the fact that law is always given, it is never produced by man himself. All evolutionary origin of law is denied. The passive includes the agent: there must always be the divine Lawgiver. This is true also of the law written in the hearts of Gentiles which is greatly blurred by the darkening effect of sin' (Lenski).

V22: **But the scripture shut up all things under sin, that the promise by faith in Jesus Christ might be given to them that believe.**

But the Scripture declares that the whole world is a prisoner of sin, (NIV) But so far from righteousness being of the law, the verdict of the law as embodied in the Scripture quoted in verse 10 [*Deut* 27.26] had exactly the opposite

effect and locked up all men under the condemnation of sin
[*Rom* 3.19].

that the promise by faith in Jesus Christ might be given
'It may be thou thinkest that all this is a preparation to thy
damnation; but it is not. For it is contrariwise a preparation
to thy salvation. For the law with a loud voice in thy heart,
proclaims thee a sinner, and threatens thee with perdition:
but the end of all this is, that Jesus Christ may become a
Saviour unto thee, so be it thou wilt come unto him, and
believe in him. For he saves no sheep, *but the lost sheep*, and
he calls not just men, but sinners to repentance' (Perkins).

to them that believe. 'The Galatians were ready to admit
that those who believed would be saved, but they doubted
whether faith *alone* was sufficient; hence the Apostle inter-
poses the limitation in reference to the thing promised ("the
promise by faith"), and virtually repeats it in reference to the
recipients. The promise was of faith, not of law; the re-
ceivers were not doers of the law, but believers' (Ellicott).

*V*23 : **But before faith came, we were kept in ward under
the law, shut up unto the faith which should afterwards
be revealed.**

**Now before this faith came, we were kept in custody
under law, being locked up with a view to the faith
that was to be revealed.** (Hendriksen) Before *the* faith
came ('note article, meaning the faith in verse 22 made possible by the historic coming of Christ the Redeemer' (A. T.
Robertson), we Jews were kept under guard by the law.
'When the Mosaic law held all the Jews under guard as it did,
it thereby stopped every mouth and declared the whole world
guilty and subject to God's judgment' (Lenski). Paul does not

deny the existence of either grace or faith under the old economy, but to those whose attention was being turned back from the grace now so fully manifested in Jesus Christ, he could only point out its privative or negative aspect. 'With a view to the faith that was to be revealed' shows that there was a beneficent purpose in this temporary bondage to the law. But if the Galatians, who enjoyed the noonday of gospel light, now reverted to the régime of law, they would lose their liberty and find themselves under its condemning constraint without hope of a reprieve [5.1].

V24: So that the law is become our tutor *to bring us* unto Christ, that we might be justified by faith.

So the law became our custodian (to conduct us) to Christ, (Hendriksen) The word translated as 'custodian' means literally 'boy-leader'. He was the man, usually a slave, whose duty it was to take the boy or youth 'to and from school and to superintend his conduct generally; he was not a "teacher" (despite the present meaning of the derivative "pedagogue")' (Arndt-Gingrich). There is no exact English equivalent, though 'schoolmaster' (AV) quite definitely conveys the wrong impression. For the word refers not to the impartation of knowledge, but to that strict discipline which was exercised by the law during the period of immaturity. Thus for the Galatians to make 'progress' after the fashion of the Judaizers would return them to a state of spiritual nonage! This custodial function of the law was not in the repression of sins; it was given to produce such convictions of guilt and helplessness as prepared for faith in Christ as the sole redeemer from its curse [v 13]. But it is important to recognize that the reference is not 'to the individual experience under the law as bringing men individually to faith in Christ. For the context makes it clear that the apostle is speaking, rather, of the historic succession of one period of revelation upon another and the displacement of the law by Christ' (Burton). [cf *vv* 23a, 25a]

that by faith we might be justified. (Hendriksen) That stern supervision was intended to lead to this happy result, 'the emphatic "by faith" serving to suggest and enhance the contrast with the non-justifying and merely pedagogic "law"' (Ellicott).

*V*25: **But now that faith is come, we are no longer under a tutor.**

But now that this faith has come we are no longer under a custodian. (Hendriksen) With this triumphant note of assurance Paul begins to remind the Galatians of the great privileges that are theirs in Christ, for to speak of the coming of *the* faith is to refer to him who is its object. They are no longer minors under austere constraint, but Christ's free men. For Christ has brought to an end the wardship of the law so that in him the church has become of age. 'God makes us adults, causes us to come of age . . . by sending His Son. Sonship as immediacy to the Father is rather different from dependence on even the best pedagogue' (G. Bertram, *TDNT*, Vol. V, p. 620). [cf 4.4–6]

*V*26: **For ye are all sons of God, through faith, in Christ Jesus.**

Paul speaks of the liberty of sonship and not of the discipline of childhood. 'The sudden change from the first to the second person plural betokens an extension in the point of view from Israel to the Gentile world. The Epistle has been dealing since 3.17 with the position of Israelites under the Law before the Advent of the Christ. But that event brought Gentiles also within the scope of God's revealed promises and of his

blessings in Christ. So the apostle turns to his converts, largely
enlisted out of Gentiles, with the assurance, "Ye are all sons of
God, whatever your antecedents". Their adoption is assumed,
as their possession of the gifts of the Spirit is assumed in 3.2.
The Spirit of adoption, of which they were conscious within
their hearts, assured them that they were sons of God [cf
Rom 8.15, 16]' (Rendall).

*V*27: **For as many of you as were baptized into Christ
did put on Christ.**

**Baptized into union with him, you have all put on
Christ as a garment.** (NEB) Why should the Galatians now
submit to circumcision when they have already clothed
themselves with Christ in baptism? 'You have all put on'
(middle voice) denotes responsible action, for in their obedience to the command of Christ they had given conscious
expression to their faith in him [*Matt* 28.19]. 'The figure of
changing garments attests to the inner spiritual change. We
strip off the clothes of the old life to be clothed with the
garments of Christ's righteousness through faith-baptism
[note the same figure in *Ps* 132.9; *Is* 61.10, 64.6; *Zech* 3.3]'
(Samuel J. Mikolaski).

*V*28: **There can be neither Jew nor Greek, there can be
neither bond nor free, there can be no male and female;
for ye all are one *man* in Christ Jesus.**

Since faith is the bond of union with Christ, differences of
race, rank, and even sex no longer divide. The thought is
not that these distinctions have ceased to exist, but that in
Christ they have ceased to matter. In this spiritual relationship, the natural son of Abraham enjoys no advantage over
the pagan Greek, the slave is in no sense the inferior of the
free man, and the man's privilege is no greater than the

woman's. It is an affirmation of religious equality, and not a programme for social reform. Paul avoided such a direct approach because he knew that men must be renewed before society could be changed. While the 'social' gospel is powerless to leaven the lump, religious revival has always resulted in social progress.

for ye are all one in Christ Jesus. (A V) 'The unity is organic, not unconscious or fortuitous juxtaposition, but like the union of all the branches with the root, and through the root with one another. There may be many disparities in gifts and graces, but there is indissoluble oneness in Christ Jesus, its only sphere, or through union to Him, its only medium' (Eadie). [*Eph* 2.15]

*V*29: **And if ye are Christ's, then are ye Abraham's seed, heirs according to promise.**

Doubt is not implied by 'if' which assumes a condition of reality. The promises of the Judaizers notwithstanding, circumcision cannot make the Gentile Galatians the heirs of Abraham. In fact that privilege is already theirs in virtue of the faith which has brought them into saving union with Christ. They are heirs, not by works of law, but 'according to promise'. 'With this last link in the chain, it becomes clear in what sense Christ could be called the seed of Abraham [*v* 16]: in a corporative sense, that is, as Head of the body and of the new covenant. Always and again this one thing is reconfirmed: that belonging to the seed of Abraham is not determined by physical descent, but by faith. Essentially, in principle, the seed of Abraham is spiritual seed' (Ridderbos).

CHAPTER FOUR

Abraham's true heirs were held under the law during the time o,
their minority, but this guardianship ceased when Christ came,
and now all believers have received the adoption of sons [vv. 1–7].
Hence it would be the height of folly if the Galatians renounced the
privileges of sonship by returning to the rudiments of legalism
[vv 8–11]. Paul touchingly recalls their former eagerness to receive
him and his gospel, which he contrasts with their inconsistency in
welcoming the Judaizers, and expresses his longing to see Christ
restored in them [vv 12–20]. The apostle finds further support for
his argument in the history of Hagar and Sarah, which illustrates
the difference between legal bondage and Christian freedom. As
the son of the servant was displaced by the son of the free woman,
so those who follow the law cannot receive the inheritance which
belongs to the children of promise [vv 21–31].

*V*1: **But I say that so long as the heir is a child, he**
differeth nothing from a bondservant though he is
lord of all; 2 but is under guardians and stewards until
the day appointed of the father.

Paul now takes up the word 'heir' to illustrate the inferior
state of the people of God under the law. For though they
were indeed the sons of God, they were sons in the time of
their minority. The child is 'his father's trueborn son. In
time he will be full owner. Meanwhile he is as subject as any

slave on the estate. There is nothing he can command for his own. He is treated and provided for as a bondman might be; put "under stewards" who manage his property, "and guardians" in charge of his person, "until the day fore-appointed of the father". This situation does not exclude, it implies fatherly affection and care on the one side, and heirship on the other. But it forbids the recognition of the heir, his investment with filial rights ... The case supposed, we observe, is not that of a *dead* father, into whose place the son steps at the proper age. A grant is made by the father *still living*, who keeps his son in pupilage till he sees fit to put him in possession of the promised estate' (G. G. Findlay). Thus the point of Paul's argument is that with the coming of Christ, the time set by the Father for investing believers with the full rights of sonship has arrived [*vv* 4–6], and the state of sub-jection to 'guardians' and 'stewards' which characterized the legal economy has been left behind.

*V*3: **So we also, when we were children, were held in bondage under the rudiments of the world:**

The R S V rendering 'elemental spirits of the universe', without even a marginal note, is regarded by Oswald T. Allis as a particularly striking example of the 'dogmatism' of that version. For as Bruce Metzger points out, 'a better translation is "rudimentary notions of the world", referring to elemen-tary religious observances [*vv* 9–10; *Col* 2.8, 20].'[1] As Paul appears to equate this expression with 'the tradition *of men*' in

1. *The New Oxford Annotated Bible*: Revised Standard Version, (O U P New York, 1973), p. 1413. Furthermore there is nothing to show that 'the cosmic elements, the stars, or related spirits etc., played any particular role in the Galatian churches', and it seems that Paul himself contributed the phrase in both Galatians and Colossians (G. Delling, TDNT, Vol. VII, pp. 684–5). See also George Eldon Ladd's note on STOICHEIA in his *Theology of the New Testament*, pp. 402–3.

Col 2.8, it seems fairly certain that the term 'world' bears an ethical meaning and refers to *mankind* as alienated from the life of God. Thus William Hendriksen interprets these 'worldly rudiments' as '*elementary teachings regarding rules and regulations, by means of which, before Christ's coming, people, both Jews and Gentiles, each in their own way, attempted by their own efforts, and in accordance with the promptings of their own fleshly (unregenerate) nature, to achieve salvation.*' The worldly man, whether he lives within or beyond the pale of special revelation, is under bondage to these regulations because he always regards salvation as a reward to be earned, and never as a gift to be received.

*V*4: **but when the fulness of the time came, God sent forth his Son, born of a woman, born under the law.**

but when the fulness of the time came, The 'servitude' of the heir lasts 'until the day appointed of the father' [*v* 2], i.e. the moment determined by God's eternal decree. Our 'spiritual bondage expires with the advent of the fulness of the time – God's set time. The nonage of the church was the duration of the Mosaic covenant. But not till the last moment of its existence, when its time was filled like a reservoir with the last drop, was it set aside, and the ripe or full age of the church commenced – "the time is fulfilled", *Mark* 1.15. The fulness of the time was also the fittest time in the world's history' (Eadie).

God sent forth his Son, This points to an eternal relationship. As the object of the Father's love, the pre-existent Son always enjoyed filial fellowship with God [2 *Cor* 8.9; *Phil* 2.6]. 'The Son's going out from God on his mission is seen in his becoming man. He did not cease to be the Son of God when he became man. He did not drop his deity, which is an impossible thought. He remained what he was and added what he had not had, namely a human nature, derived out of a woman, a human mother. He became the God-man' (Lenski).

born of a woman, In accordance with the divine decree, the Son of God entered the world of men by being 'born of a woman'. The apostle does not say, 'born of a virgin', for he is stressing the humiliation of Christ, his likeness to us, a likeness which he voluntarily assumed for our redemption. 'Paul is thinking not of the difference, but of the identity of Christ's birth and our own. We are carried back to Bethlehem. We see Jesus a babe lying in his mother's arms – *God's Son a human infant*, drawing his life from a weak woman!' (Findlay).

born under the law, It was with the express purpose of liberating those who were under the curse of the law that Christ by his birth became subject to all the law's demands. As the surety of a sinful people he came to pay their debt to the law of God, not only to fulfil all its *precepts* as our representative [*Matt* 3.15, 5.17], but also to exhaust its *penalty* as our substitute [3.13].

V5: **that he might redeem them that were under the law, that we might receive the adoption of sons.**

These two final clauses set forth two gracious purposes of God in the plan of salvation. They correspond to the clauses of the previous verse in an inverted order (chiasmus): 'The Son of God was born a man that we might receive the adoption of sons; He was born under the law that he might redeem them which were under the law' (Lightfoot).

The first gracious purpose of God was the removal of the great hindrance to our adoption. The primary reference is to the Mosaic law. Jesus was born under that law which gave the most perfect and exact expression to the claims of God upon man. It was by exhausting the curse of the highest law that Christ redeemed his people from all bondage to any kind of law [3.13]. Hence his sacrifice has ushered in the era of liberty from which there can be no reversion to the tutelary bondage of the Mosaic covenant. 'The description *under Law* includes Gentiles as well as Jews: for though they had not *the Law*, they were not without Law to God [cf *Rom* 2.14]: they had indeed been expressly specified in 3.14 as included in the redemption from the curse of the Law' (Rendall).

The second gracious purpose of God was the bestowal of the unspeakable privilege of our adoption into the family of God [1 *John* 3.1]. He who was the Son *by nature* willingly took the form of a servant, so that we who were by nature the servants of sin might become sons by the adoption *of grace*! His Father is now our Father, for he has ascended to heaven not only as the natural Son returned home to the Father, but also as the triumphant Son of Man who took his place in glory on our behalf [*John* 20.17; *Heb* 2.11, 12].

*V*6: **And because ye are sons, God sent forth the Spirit of his Son into our hearts, crying, Abba, Father.**

To prove that you are sons, God has sent into our hearts the Spirit of his Son, (NEB) The Galatians must realize that the presence of the Spirit is the proof of their adoption [3.2]. They are not minors under discipline, but have been endowed with all the rights and privileges of sonship. As God sent forth his Son to accomplish redemption [*v* 4], so he sent forth 'the Spirit of his Son' to apply its benefits to the hearts of his people. The significance of this title, which occurs only here in the New Testament, is that it shows that the activity of the Spirit is never divorced from the Son whom he was sent into the world to glorify [*John*

16.14]. This means that the objective blessings of justification cannot be separated from their realization through the gift of the Spirit. The passage affords no encouragement whatever to any conception of a two-stage faith which relegates justification to the 'primary' stage of Christian experience, and urges believers to strive after the 'higher life' of the Spirit. It is the express teaching of the apostle that this assurance of sonship is certified to believers by the Spirit in conversion, and not in some subsequent experience [cf *Eph* 1.13 NIV].

crying, Abba, Father. The research of Joachim Jeremias has shown that though the Jews never dared to address God in this intimate way, Jesus always used this form (except in the cry of dereliction on the cross, *Matt* 27.46), and taught his disciples to do the same. It is only in virtue of the new relationship given by *God* through the *Son* and actualized by the *Spirit* that men can joyfully cry, 'Abba, dear Father'. Hence the mere fact that Gentile Christians accepted this Aramaic word into their prayers 'shows how conscious they were of the new element which had been given them in the cry of "Abba"' (J. Jeremias, *The Prayers of Jesus*, p. 65).

> *'Abba, Father', Lord, we call Thee –*
> *Hallowed Name! – from day to day;*
> *'Tis Thy children's right to know Thee,*
> *None but children 'Abba' say.*
> *This high glory we inherit,*
> *Thy free gift through Jesus' blood;*
> *God the Spirit, with our spirit,*
> *Witnesseth we're sons of God.*
> Robert Hawker

*V*7: **So that thou art no longer a bondservant, but a son; and if a son, then an heir through God.**

Thus the evidence of sonship is to be seen in that filial consciousness which is produced by the gift of the Spirit. Paul 'changes to the singular to drive the point home to each one. The spiritual experience [3.2] has set each one free. Each is now a son and heir' (Robertson).

through God. This 'carries to a climax the emphatic repetition of "God" observed in *vv* 4 and 6. "*God* sent his Son" into the world; "*God* sent" in turn "his Son's Spirit into your hearts". God then, and no other, has bestowed your inheritance. It is yours by his fiat. Who dares challenge it?' (Findlay).

*V*8: **Howbeit at that time, not knowing God, ye were in bondage to them that by nature are no gods:**

Paul here contrasts the former ignorance of the Galatians with their present knowledge. Now that they have come to know the one living God they enjoy the liberty of sons, but before their conversion they were held in abject bondage by imaginary deities of man's invention. The phrase 'by nature are no gods' determinatively discriminates between the true God and all other so-called gods. 'False worship given to God, presupposeth a false opinion of God: and a false opinion of God sets up an idol, or false god, in the room of the true God. For it is not sufficient to conceive some true things of God, but we must precisely conceive him, as he hath revealed himself, without addition or detraction. And thus did the wisest of the Galatians worship false gods' (Perkins). [1 *Cor* 8.4–6]

*V*9: **but now that ye have come to know God, or rather to be known by God, how turn ye back again to the weak and beggarly rudiments, whereunto ye desire to be in bondage over again?**

Paul corrects himself since the Galatians had only come to know God through his prior knowledge of them. Salvation is wholly of God 'whose gracious fore-knowing and fore-appointing of us to eternal life is the ground and foundation of our illumination and conversion, our love to him a reflex of his love to us' (John Trapp).

but now . . . how turn ye back again? 'By *rudiments* we are to understand Circumcision, the Jewish Sacrifices, and all the ceremonies of the law of *Moses*. And it may not seem strange, that they are called impotent and beggarly rudiments. For they must be considered three ways, with Christ, without Christ, and against Christ. With Christ, when they are considered as types and figures of Christ to come, and as signs of grace by divine institution for the time of the Old Testament. Without Christ, when they are used only for custom, whether before or after the death of Christ. Against Christ, when they are esteemed as meritorious causes of salvation, and the justification of a sinner is placed in them, either in whole or in part: as though Christ alone were not sufficient. In this respect *Paul* calls them impotent and beggarly rudiments.

'And *Paul* having said, that the Galatians returned again to the rudiments of the law, in the next words he shows how they do it: namely, by *serving them again*. They served or yielded service to them three ways: In opinion, because they judged them to be necessary parts of God's worship, and means of their salvation. In conscience, because they subjected their consciences to them. In affection, because they placed part of their affiance in them for their justification and salvation.

'It may be demanded, how the Galatians can be said to return again to the rudiments of the law, and serve them again, that were never used to them before? *Answer*. In the speech of *Paul* there is that which is called *Catachresis*, that is, a kind of speaking somewhat improper in respect of fineness and elegancy. The like we have, *Ruth* 1.22, when *Ruth* is said to return to Judea with *Naomi*; and yet she was never there before. Nevertheless, the speech in sense is most significant and proper. For *Paul* (no doubt) signifies hereby, that when the Galatians subjected themselves to the rudiments of the law, and placed their salvation in part even in them, they did in effect and in truth as much as return again to their old superstitions, and serve again their false gods' (Perkins).

*V*10: **Ye observe days, and months, and seasons, and years.**

Paul sees in the eagerness of the Galatians to embrace the legalistic observance of Jewish religious festivals a conspicuous example of their sad decline from the freedom of the gospel. It seems reasonable to assume with Burton that the Judaizers had adopted the adroit course of first presenting to them the least objectionable requirements of the Jewish law, and that they were now urging them to receive circumcision [cf 5.2, 3, 12; 6.12, 13]. Since Paul is rebuking Gentiles for subjecting themselves to Jewish ordinances *and that with a view to acquiring merit before God*, it is evident that the verse furnishes no argument against the obligation to observe the Christian Sabbath. 'Yet all superstitious observation of days is unlawful, as being here condemned, either expressly or by consequence' (Fergusson). [*Col* 2.16]

*V*11: **I am afraid of you, lest by any means I have bestowed labour upon you in vain.**

I am afraid for you, lest I might have expended my labour on you in vain. (Arndt-Gingrich) Although Paul hopes that the Galatians have not heard the gospel in vain [3.4], their present conduct certainly puts a large question mark over the effectiveness of his work in their midst. In thus frankly expressing his fear for their safety, he intends to rouse them from their legal stupor to the evangelical grace of repentance. 'There is something peculiarly affecting in these simple words of the apostle. He had laboured, laboured too with apparent success; but now, through the exertion of false teachers, the fruits of his labour seem in extreme hazard of being completely blasted. How happy would it be for Christ's church if ministers in general were of the apostle's spirit – "jealous over their people with a godly jealousy!"' (John Brown). [2 *Cor* 11.2]

*V*12a: **I beseech you, brethren, become as I *am* for I also *am become* as ye *are*.**

Even to contemplate the possibility of his having laboured among the Galatians to no purpose is so distressing to Paul that he breaks into a passionate personal appeal [*vv* 12–20]. '"As I, though a zealous Jew by birth [1.14], in my life among you cast out Jewish habits, so do ye; for I am become as ye are" – viz., in not observing legal ordinances. "My laying them aside among Gentiles shows that I regard them as *not at all contributing to justification or sanctification*. Do you regard them in the same light, and act accordingly". His observing the law among the Jews was not inconsistent with this, for he did so to win them, without compromising principle [1 *Cor* 9.20, 21]. But the Galatian Gentiles, by adopting legal ordinances, showed they regarded them as needful for salvation' (Fausset).

*V*12b: **Ye did me no wrong: 13 but ye know that because of an infirmity of the flesh I preached the gospel unto you the first time: 14 and that which was a temptation to you in my flesh ye despised not, nor rejected; but ye received me as an angel of God, *even* as Christ Jesus.**

Despite the distressing circumstances under which Paul brought the gospel to the Galatians, he reminds them that

[85]

they did him no harm at that time. For though the sight of a man in such bodily weakness could well have caused them to turn away from him and his message in contempt, they had received him so warmly that they might have been welcoming an angel of God, or even Christ himself! How sadly different was their attitude towards him now!

We have no means of knowing the nature of Paul's infirmity, still less whether it is to be connected with his 'thorn in the flesh' [2 *Cor* 12.7]. But evidently illness forced him to change his travel plans, for it was 'because of a physical ailment' (Arndt-Gingrich) that he came to preach in their area. There is also uncertainty over the meaning of the phrase 'the first time'. It could either mean 'originally' (NEB) or 'on that former occasion' (Hendriksen), pointing to the first of two visits. Perhaps the first alternative is preferable, though the second is not incompatible with the sequence of events suggested in the Introduction, for if that view is correct Paul would have visited the Galatians *twice* on the first missionary journey [cf *Acts* 14.21].

V15: **Where then is that gratulation of yourselves? for I bear you witness, that, if possible, ye would have plucked out your eyes and given them to me.**

Where then is your felicitation of yourselves? (Lightfoot) Paul asks the Galatians what has become of the happiness they once felt in his ministry. They then congratulated themselves because the apostle had brought them the good news of God's free grace in Christ. But they lost their joy when they began to give heed to the law-message of the Judaizers. The question thus underlines the folly of exchanging the blessings of grace for the treadmill of works. It is precarious to assume from the second part of the verse that Paul was afflicted with some form of eye disease like ophthalmia. He simply means that at the time of their conversion they thought so highly of him, they would have deemed no sacrifice too great to make on his behalf. 'For had it been possible to benefit me by plucking out the most precious member of your body, you would have done so!' [cf Ps 17.8; Matt 5.29]

V16: **So then am I become your enemy, by telling you the truth?**

Is it possible that the Galatians who once regarded themselves as greatly blessed in knowing Paul have now come to think of him as their enemy? Is he their enemy simply because he is too good a friend to refrain from telling them the truth they would prefer not to hear? The important lesson which this verse teaches us is that we cannot be selective with the truth of God. We cannot choose what we like and reject what we dislike of the apostolic teaching. 'No, the apostles of Jesus Christ have authority in everything they teach, whether we happen to like it or not' (John Stott).

V17: **They zealously seek you in no good way; nay, they desire to shut you out, that ye may seek them.**

These people are zealously courting you for no commendable purpose: on the contrary, they want to isolate you, in order that you may zealously court them. (Hendriksen) Paul's genuine concern for the spiritual welfare of his converts is in sharp contrast to the selfish and sinister motives of his rivals for their affections, the Judaizers, whom he does not condescend to name here. While they now pay court to the Galatians, their intentions are far from honourable. For when the churches have been cut off from all contact with the apostle of their liberty, they will become entirely dependent upon these taskmasters of bondage. Such is ever the technique of the cultist!

*V*18: **But it is good to be zealously sought in a good matter at all times, and not only when I am present with you.**

Now (it is) commendable to be zealously courted in connection with a commendable cause (and this) always, (Hendriksen) Paul here gives abstract expression to a truth which must command their ready assent. Zealous courting is good provided the suitor pursues an honourable course in an honourable way. Now whereas the Judaizers had cast dishonour upon the Galatians by seeking to seduce them from the truth for their own selfish gain, Paul had brought honour to them by courting them with honourable intentions in a supremely honourable cause, the gospel. And what is honourable at one time must also be honourable at all times!

and not only when I am present with you. Paul now lets the Galatians see that this principle applies no less to the wooed than it does to the wooer. For a faithful suitor demands constancy in his beloved whether he happens to be present or absent. Yet no sooner had Paul turned his back than the fickle Galatians began to respond to the dishonourable over-tures of those who designed to pervert the purity of their faith. 'If the Apostle be thus jealous, how much more then is Christ himself jealous, who hath espoused himself to his Church? This plainly shows, that he cannot brook either partner, or deputy. And therefore his sacrifice on the cross must stand without the sacrifice of the Mass, his intercession without the intercession of Saints, his merits without the merit of works, his satisfaction without any satisfaction of ours. He will have the heart alone, and all the heart, or nothing: and he will not give any part of his honour to any other' (Perkins).

*V*19: **My little children, of whom I am again in travail until Christ be formed in you –**

My little children, This mode of address so common in *John* is not used elsewhere by Paul. Here the diminutive is expressive both of 'the tenderness of the Apostle and the feebleness of his converts' (Lightfoot). His spontaneous outburst of tender affection for his erring children has the irresistible appeal of being completely genuine. Their spiritual birth had once involved him in painful travail, but now their threatened defection has brought on those birth-pangs for the second time! Not as though they needed a second conversion, but rather that Christ might be so completely formed in them that they would be for ever immune from the insidious germs of false doctrine. He is not satisfied to see them assume a mask of Christ; his eager desire is that they may fully know the inner reality of Christ living within their hearts. As Calvin well says, 'If ministers wish to do any good, let them labour to form Christ, not to form themselves, in their hearers'. Hence they must labour so to teach the Word of God 'in demonstration of the Spirit and of power' that men may come to know the Christ of whom it testifies.

*V*20: **but I could wish to be present with you now, and to change my tone; for I am perplexed about you.**

This upsurge of affection for his converts makes Paul wish he were now present with them so that he could change his tone. For with the obstacle of distance removed, he would be able to assure them of his love even as he sought to disabuse them of their errors. 'Paul could put his heart into his voice. The pen stands between them. He knew the power of his voice on their hearts. He had tried it before' (Robertson). He confesses his perplexity as he wonders how best to continue his exhortation, and restore their faith in the one gospel from which they had so sadly declined.

V21: **Tell me, ye that desire to be under the law, do ye not hear the law?**

At this point Paul does indeed change his tone. 'He will tell his "children" a story!' (Findlay). He challenges those who desire to be under the law to hear what the law (i.e. the Pentateuch) is really saying to them through the history of the two sons of Abraham. He would have them learn that the law has in it far more than the specific commands of a vanished ceremonialism; it also contains in germ the grace that is now openly proclaimed to them in the gospel. Thus the spiritual lessons which the apostle draws from this story are firmly based upon the historical facts. He simply makes patent what is latent in the narrative.

V22: **For it is written, that Abraham had two sons, one by the handmaid, and one by the free woman.**

This is not a direct quotation but a summary of the facts (recorded in *Gen* 16 and 21) which show that it is possible to be a son of Abraham in more than one sense. For Abraham had two sons, one by the slave woman and one by the free woman. And what they were by birth made all the difference to their respective destinies. Neither the unbelief which proposed its own fulfilment of God's promise nor the opposition of the natural seed could frustrate God's elective purpose of grace [*Gen* 16.2; 21.9]. So though he was the elder son, the inheritance was not for Ishmael, because unlike Isaac, he was not born free.

V23: **Howbeit the *son* by the handmaid is born after the flesh; but the *son* by the free woman *is born* through promise.**

Not only were these the sons of different mothers, but there was also a significant difference in the manner of their begetting. The son who was born after the ordinary course of nature is here contrasted with the son who was born through promise. One birth was natural, the other was supernatural in that God intervened in a miraculous way to enable Abraham and Sarah to have Isaac long after all hope of any purely human fulfilment of the promise had been extinguished [*Gen* 21.7; *Rom* 4.19–21; *Heb* 11.11]. This child who was brought to birth by the exercise of divine power therefore becomes the fitting symbol of all who are supernaturally born of the Spirit [cf *v* 29].

*V*24: **Which things contain an allegory: for these *women* are two covenants; one from mount Sinai, bearing children unto bondage, which is Hagar.**

Which things contain an allegory: This means 'to express or explain one thing under the image of another' (Ellicott). Calvin castigates Origen and those like him for having 'seized this occasion of twisting Scripture this way and that, away from the genuine sense. For they inferred that the literal sense is too meagre and poor and that beneath the bark of the letter there lie deeper mysteries which cannot be extracted but by hammering out allegories'. This single example of allegorizing by the apostle therefore affords no lawful precedent to give our imaginations free rein with the text of Scripture. Paul was inspired; we are not! Moreover, Paul's use of allegory is very different from Philo's ingenious speculations. 'The simple historical facts are not explained away as if they had been portions of a mere allegory, like the persons and events in Bunyan's *Pilgrim*; but these facts are invested with a new meaning as portraying great spiritual truths, and such truths they were intended and moulded to symbolize' (Eadie).

[91]

for these *women* are two covenants; The free woman represents the Abrahamic covenant of promise and the slave woman represents the Sinaitic covenant of law. As Paul sees these women in terms of two contrasted series of concepts, the differences between them can be grasped more easily if they are arranged in parallel columns:

Hagar, the slave woman	Sarah, the free woman
Ishmael, the natural child, 'born after the flesh'	Isaac, the spiritual heir, 'born after the Spirit'
The Old Covenant	The New Covenant
The earthly Jerusalem	The heavenly Jerusalem
The bondage of the law	The freedom of the gospel

one from Mount Sinai, bearing children unto bondage, Although God 'gave his law to Israel in a context of grace, that law was unable to save anyone. Besides, when it is, nevertheless, viewed as a force by means of which a person achieves deliverance and salvation, as the Jews and Judaizers actually viewed it, then it enslaves. It then not only leaves men in their bondage but more and more adds to their heavy burden' (Hendriksen) [see comment on 3.12, 23; cf Matt 11.28, 29; Rom 8.15]

which is Hagar. With this shattering identification Paul lets his infatuated readers know that they may indeed become the sons of Abraham by means of law. Yes, 'the Law will make you his sons by Hagar, whose home is Sinai – not Israelites, but *Ishmaelites*!' (Findlay).

V25: **Now this Hagar is mount Sinai in Arabia, and answereth to the Jerusalem that now is: for she is in bondage with her children.**

Now Hagar stands for Mount Sinai in Arabia (NIV) 'The thought "Hagar" (not the word and not the woman as such, but the thought of bondage suggested by her) corresponds to Mount Sinai, situated in a desert land and far away from the land of promise generally, and Jerusalem in particular' (Williams).

and corresponds to the present city of Jerusalem, (NIV) Thus Hagar, Sinai, and present-day Jerusalem all belong together in the same rank or category. It was Sinai and not Canaan that Paul saw in Jerusalem, for it was no longer the capital of the land of *promise* but had become the metropolis of *legalism*. A terrible indictment indeed!

for she is in bondage with her children. This is the 'justification of the parallelism just affirmed between Hagar and Jerusalem. As Hagar, a slave, bore children that by that birth passed into slavery, so the Jerusalem that now is and her children, viz., all the adherents of legalistic Judaism which has its centre in Jerusalem, are in bondage to law' (Burton).

*V*26: **But the Jerusalem that is above is free, which is our mother.**

In his haste to apply the truth Paul does not stop to complete the figure by naming Sarah as the other mother. The contrast he draws is not between *present* bondage and *future* bliss, since he is showing the Galatians that believers even now enjoy that liberty which descends to them from Jerusalem above. In other words, the 'eschatological salvation is not awaited in an indefinite future but has come already. We who believe in Christ are children of our mother, the Jerusalem which is above, *v* 31' (E. Lohse, *TDNT*, Vol. VII, p. 337).

'What he calls heavenly is not shut up in heaven, nor are we to seek for it outside the world. For the Church is spread over the whole world and is a pilgrim on the earth. Why then is it said to be from heaven? Because it originates in heavenly grace. For the sons of God are born, not of flesh and blood, but by the power of the Holy Spirit. The heavenly Jerusalem, which derives its origin from heaven and dwells above by faith, is the mother of believers' (Calvin).

*V*27: **For it is written,**
   Rejoice, thou barren that bearest not;
   Break forth and cry, thou that travailest not:
   For more are the children of the desolate than
      of her that hath the husband.

That the glory of the church far surpasses the temporary favours once vouchsafed to an earthly Zion is proved by an appeal to *Isaiah* 54.1 according to the Septuagint (the most influential Greek translation of the Old Testament). The preceding verses in *Isaiah*, ch 52.13–53.12, clearly teach that the grounds of this rejoicing are found in the redemptive accomplishments of the Lord Jesus Christ. It is because Paul sees the barren Sarah and exiled Israel as fitting symbols of the fructifying power of the divine promise that he aptly applies the passage to the church's experience of the power of her exalted Saviour.

'Paul calls the church barren because her children are not born by means of the Law or works or any human efforts or powers but in the Holy Spirit through the Word of faith. This is purely a matter of being born, not of doing any works. Those who are prolific, on the other hand, labour and strain greatly in travail; this is purely a matter of doing works, not of giving birth. But those who try to achieve the status of sons and heirs by the righteousness of the Law or by their own righteousness are slaves, who will never receive the inheritance even though they work themselves to death with their great effort; for they are trying, contrary to the will of God, to achieve by their own works what God wants to grant to believers by sheer grace for Christ's sake. Believers do good works; but they do not become sons and heirs through this, for this has been granted to them by their birth. Now that they have become sons for Christ's sake, they glorify God with their good deeds and help their neighbour' (Luther).

*V*28: **Now we, brethren, as Isaac was, are children of promise.**

Now you, brothers, like Isaac, are children of promise. (NIV) The implication is that if the Galatians insist on behaving like those born 'after the flesh' they will forfeit the status that is theirs by grace, for they are 'children' only by virtue of the promise. 'In Isaac this became apparent from the circumstances of birth; in believers it becomes apparent in the quickening, the regenerating, of the Spirit [cf *v* 29]. But in both instances, God's power and sovereign grace is the cause of the birth . . . The household of Abraham is the prototype of the church of God. The promise which accrued to him is the secret of the maintenance of the church. Ishmael's and Isaac's birth represents the two attitudes towards the promise: that of human self-vindication and that of faith' (Ridderbos).

*V*29: **But as then he that was born after the flesh persecuted him** *that was born* **after the Spirit, so also it is now.**

Paul next shows that Ishmael's mockery of the infant Isaac gave evidence of such malice that it could be called nothing less than a persecution of the heir of promise. The reference is to *Gen* 21.9 which should read 'laughing at him' (NEB) and *not* 'playing' with him (RSV). It would seem that Ishmael made Isaac's name ('laughter'), which was given to him in holy joy, the butt for his unholy ridicule. Thus Isaac 'was laughter to his mother in one sense, but to his brother in a

[95]

very different sense – the one laughed for him, the other at him' (Eadie).

so also it is now. The Judaizers doubtless held up the gospel of God's grace to the same ridicule. 'The persecution of the church by Judaism gave proof of the Ishmaelite spirit, the carnal animus by which it was possessed. A religion of externalism naturally becomes repressive. It knows not "the demonstration of the Spirit"; it has "confidence in the flesh". It relies on outward means for the propagation of its faith; and naturally resorts to the secular arm. The Inquisition and the Auto-da-fé are a not unfitting accompaniment of the gorgeous ceremonial of the Mass. Ritualism and priestly autocracy go hand in hand' (Findlay). [cf 2 *Cor* 10.3–5]

*V*30: **Howbeit what saith the scripture? Cast out the handmaid and her son: for the son of the handmaid shall not inherit with the son of the free woman.**

Paul's question challenges his converts to apply this Scripture to the deplorable crisis in the Galatian churches. Sarah's demand for the expulsion of Hagar and Ishmael was a truly prophetic word, for it gave expression to the sentence of God [*Gen* 21.10, 12]. As the Scripture is a living word, it still pronounces this same verdict upon all those who have no higher birth than Ishmael's. So that all the Galatians will accomplish by succumbing to the blandishments of the Judaizers is their own exclusion from any share of the inheritance of grace.

'The Law and the Gospel cannot co-exist; the Law must disappear before the Gospel. It is scarcely possible to estimate the strength of conviction and depth of prophetic insight which this declaration implies. The Apostle thus confidently sounds the death-knell of Judaism at a time when one-half of Christendom clung to the Mosaic law with a jealous affection little short of frenzy, and while the Judaic party seemed, to be growing in influence and was strong enough, even in the Gentile churches of his own founding, to undermine his influence and endanger his life. The truth which to us appears a truism must then have been regarded as paradox' (Lightfoot).

V31: Wherefore, brethren, we are not children of a handmaid, but of the free woman.

The practical conclusion the Galatians are to draw from this allegory is now expressed in the simplest form. Since they are children of the free woman they must act accordingly, and not submit to any form of bondage: '"not of *any* bond-woman" whether of Judaism or some form of heathenism, for there are *many*, but "but of *the* free woman, the lawful spouse, the Church of Christ, which is *one*"' (Lightfoot).

CHAPTER FIVE

Paul warns the Galatians not to forfeit their freedom in Christ, for if they consent to circumcision they would exchange justifying grace for the condemnation of the law [vv 1–6]. He reminds them of their good beginning through believing the preaching of the cross, and denounces the preachers of circumcision who are now leading them astray from the truth [vv 7–12]. Yet liberty must not be confused with licence, and they are to use their freedom to serve one another in love [vv 13–15]. To walk by the Spirit is to be free from the lust of the flesh, but they must desist from the works of the flesh if they would bring forth the fruit of the Spirit [vv 16–26].

Vi: For freedom did Christ set us free: stand fast therefore, and be not entangled again in a yoke of bondage.

The ASV rightly makes a separate paragraph of this verse, for it serves the double function of summing up the whole of Paul's doctrinal argument [chs 3, 4], and of providing the point of transition for his ethical argument [chs 5, 6].

For freedom did Christ set us free: In making this emphatic affirmation Paul was not indulging in needless repetition, for the Galatians were in dire danger of despising their birthright. The statement virtually amounts to the challenge: 'Did Christ set us free that we might be slaves? No, but that we might be free!' He thus blames them for overlooking the

[98]

purpose of Christ's great sacrifice, for it was to liberate guilty sinners from the curse of the law that he died and rose again [3.13; 22–25]. This freedom became a reality in their experience through the power of the Spirit, who had invested them with the liberty of sons by applying the all–sufficient merit of that redemptive accomplishment to their hearts [3.2; 4.6]. Hence their falling back into bondage was 'inexplicable and inexcusable' (Ridderbos). As the nature of this freedom is defined by all that has gone before, so all that follows shows that it must not be confused with lawless licence.

stand fast therefore, and be not entangled again in a yoke of bondage. The whole of the apostle's appeal to the Galatians is contained in this urgent charge to maintain their freedom, and to stand firm against the efforts of the Judaizers to bring them again under a yoke of bondage. The force of 'again' is well noted by Lightfoot: 'Having escaped from the slavery of Heathenism, they would fain bow to the slavery of Judaism' [cf 4.9]. Those who have been liberated by Christ to serve him in perfect freedom must not yield themselves in servile submission to *any* such yoke of slavery [cf Matt 11.29, 30 with 23.4].

*V*2: **Behold, I Paul say unto you, that if ye receive circumcision, Christ will profit you nothing.**

'Behold' is a sharp summons to pay heed to a warning of the highest moment, the unique authority of which is demonstrated by the emphatic 'I Paul'. He will not mince his words, for the salvation of his converts is at stake. Already they have surrendered much of their freedom to the demands of the Judaizers [4.10], and now they are on the brink of submitting to that rite which would be 'the sacrament of their excision from Christ' (Huxtable cited by Findlay). They cannot have Christ *and* circumcision; they must choose circumcision *or*

Christ. As Ridderbos points out, this does not mean that circumcision is of itself an impediment to Christ, but the legalist demand that those who were never subject to the law of Moses should receive it *as a condition for obtaining salvation* perverted the gospel by challenging the sufficiency of Christ's work. 'Many do profess Christ who shall receive no saving advantage by him, especially they who rely upon any thing besides him, or jointly with him, as the meritorious cause of their salvation: for saith he, "If ye be circumcised, Christ shall profit you nothing"' (Fergusson).

*V*3: **Yea, I testify again to every man that receiveth circumcision, that he is a debtor to do the whole law.**

'Again' repeats the warning of the previous verse. But this time Paul solemnly assures every man who is contemplating circumcision that this act will not only sever his connection with Christ, but will also place him under an obligation to keep the whole law. He who is not content to owe his salvation entirely to grace becomes a debtor to do the whole law, which is 'impossible for man to keep in part, much less *wholly* [James 2.10]; yet none can be justified by it, unless he keep it *wholly* [3.10]' (Fausset).

*V*4: **Ye are severed from Christ, ye who would be justified by the law; ye are fallen away from grace.**

The severity of the apostle's language is meant to disabuse the Galatians of their misguided enthusiasm for the law. For to seek justification by one's own works according to law, implies a severance from Christ as the provider of righteousness, and a non-reliance upon God's grace as the source of our salvation. 'Christ's method of justification is wholly of grace, and those who rely on law and merit are in opposition to grace – are fallen out of it. The clause has really no bearing on the doctrine of the perseverance of the saints, or on their possible apostasy' (Eadie). Those who are saints take heed of such warnings and persevere in their calling; those who are not often show it by publicly separating themselves from that domain of grace to which they never truly belonged.

V5: **For we through the Spirit by faith wait for the hope of righteousness.**

for it is by faith that 'we' wait in the Spirit for the righteousness we hope for; (Moffatt) Far from seeking to supplement our faith by any *work* [*v* 4], 'we' who believe God's promise simply *wait* in the Spirit for the hoped-for righteousness. Thus the Spirit who unites us with Christ enables us to live in earnest expectation of our final salvation. According to the New Testament believers do not wait for a second experience of the Holy Spirit, imperfectly received in conversion. They rather wait 'in the Spirit' for the inheritance, which is assured to them through their present experience of the Spirit [cf *Rom* 5.5; 8.23f; *Eph* 1.13f; 4.30].

Although believers are already justified, their righteous standing before God has yet to be revealed, and this is therefore still the object of their hope [*Col* 1.5; *2 Tim* 4.8]. But legal justification has no future, and is present only in the legalist's imagination. 'Justification by faith is present, and also stretches in sure "hope" on to eternity. Righteousness, now the believer's hidden possession, shall then *shine out* as glory' [*Matt* 13.43; *Col* 3.3, 4] (Fausset).

V6: **For in Christ Jesus neither circumcision availeth anything, nor uncircumcision; but faith working through love.**

For in Christ Jesus This verse is of outstanding importance since it establishes the spiritual nature of the Christian faith.

As the very source of Paul's life was union with Christ (he uses the phrase 'in Christ' some 160 times in his letters), he could no longer define religion in terms of external marks and carnal ordinances [cf *Phil* 3.4–6]. Hence he speaks here of that vital *spiritual* relationship in which faith is all-important, and the externals of the *flesh* are a matter of complete indifference. The phrase shows that it takes more than a formal assent to certain truths about Christ to make a man a Christian, for it is only through union with a *living* Saviour that Christianity becomes in the truest sense of the word a *living* religion.

neither circumcision availeth anything, nor uncircumcision; 'The uncircumcised has nothing to boast of over the circumcised; if both be in Christ, their condition is equal – is influenced neither by the presence of the mere external rite, nor by the want of it' (Eadie).

but faith working through love. 'This is the new *creature*; [6.15]. He joined *hope* with *faith*; now he joins with it *love*. In these the whole of *Christianity* consists' (Bengel). For though the law commands love, only faith can beget love, and thus provide us with the moral dynamic to fulfil the law [*v* 14; *Rom* 13.8–10]. As Lightfoot points out, these words bridge over the gulf which seems to separate the language of Paul and James, since both see faith as 'a principle of practical energy, as opposed to a barren, inactive theory'. Paul praises the true faith which is fruitful in every good work, whereas James condemns the false faith which is barren of any good work [*James* 2.20].

*V*7: **Ye were running well; who hindered you that ye should not obey the truth?**

When the Galatians were running well they were obeying the truth. Their right belief was shown in right conduct. But the Judaizers had hindered them, for their preaching of works had broken up the highway of free grace and halted their progress [cf 3.2f; *Heb* 12.1]. 'The man who yields his mind to the influence of the truth as it is in Jesus, finds all he needs in Christ – he does not go about to establish a way of justification of his own, but submits to God's method of justification, through the faith of Christ. All halting in the Christian course originates here. While the mind yields itself up to the influence of the truth, the Christian runs well; but whenever this influence is resisted, he is hindered' (John Brown).

*V*8: **This persuasion** *came* **not of him that calleth you.**

that persuasion, that draws you away from the truth, **does not come from him who calls you.** (Arndt-Gingrich) 'The Judaistic arts and arguments were not in harmony with the effectual calling of God. The one is – persuasion – art and arguments – on merely human and specious principles; the other is "calling", the summons of God to life and truth in Christ. The apostle goes back in idea to "Who hindered you?" – the Judaizers are present to his mind from this question on through several verses and to the end of the twelfth verse. It is their work which he thus pictures; their "persuasion" was the preaching of another gospel, the bewitching of the Galatians' (Eadie). [3.1]

*V*9: **A little leaven leaveneth the whole lump.**

This is a proverbial saying which Paul uses in a different connection in 1 *Cor* 5.6. There it refers to the leavening effect of one man's sin upon the whole church; here it is applied to the doctrine of the Judaizers. 'A little legalism, mixed with the gospel, corrupts its purity. To add ordinances and works in the least degree to justification by faith, is to undermine *the whole*' (Fausset). The danger for the Galatians in accepting their *persons* lay in receiving their false *principles*. It is the Word of God, and not a pleasing presence, that is the touchstone by which every teacher is to be judged [*Is* 8.20]. And the contemporary church will never recover the pure gospel until she learns to reject those who bring her a different gospel, even though they may have the ability to present error in an attractive guise [cf 2 *Cor* 11.13–15]

V10: I have confidence to you-ward in the Lord, that ye will be none otherwise minded : but *he* that troubleth you shall bear his judgment, whosoever he be.

I on my part am persuaded in the Lord with respect to you, that you will not adopt a different view (from mine). In spite of the ready reception the Galatians had given the Judaizers, Paul believes that disenchantment will follow this temporary success. He has confidence that his converts will adhere to the one true gospel. This persuasion 'rests not on any innate goodness of theirs, but solely on *their* and *his* relation to Christ, *their* and also *his* Lord. It is that Lord who, having begun a good work in the Galatians, will carry it on toward completion' (Hendriksen). [*Phil* 1.6]

but he that troubleth you shall bear his judgment, whosoever he be. The singular 'he' does not designate a particular person, but simply supposes that what is true of an individual is also true of the class he represents. For anyone who burdens the church with false teaching shall not escape being burdened with a crushing judgment. In that day all who have recklessly perverted the gospel shall discover to their eternal sorrow that 'it is no light thing to scatter the leaven of false doctrine' (Lenski).

V11: But I, brethren, if I still preach circumcision, why am I still persecuted? then hath the stumbling-block of the cross been done away.

Apparently the Judaizers had even appealed to the 'example' of Paul in their attempts to persuade the Galatians to receive circumcision. But if he were *still* (temporal: as he was before his conversion) the advocate for circumcision, why is he *still* (logical: in that case) being persecuted? That he proclaims a very different message is proved by the fact that his preaching does not attract the applause of the circumcised, but provokes them to such fury that they persecute him in every place.

This leads to the ironical conclusion that the offensiveness of the cross, that which aroused such violent opposition, has been removed. The persecuted apostle was, however, the living proof that the offence of the cross remained, as did its power to save [6.17]. He resolutely refused to adapt his preaching to the prejudices of his kinsmen after the flesh, and presented them with a crucified Messiah as the supreme fulfilment of their national hope. 'Worldly Wiseman, of the town of Carnal Policy, turns Christian out of the narrow way of the Cross to the house of legality. But the way to it was up a mountain, which, as Christian advanced, threatened to fall on and crush him, amidst lightning flashes from the mountain ('Pilgrim's Progress': *Heb* 12.18–21)' (Fausset).

*V*12 : **I would that they that unsettle you would even go beyond circumcision.**

I wish those who unsettle you would mutilate themselves! (RSV)

This may not be watered down to a wish that the Judaizers might be cut off from the communion of the church. It is rather an expression of deep disgust with those who are unsettling the Galatians with an emasculated message: these people had better complete the process by following the example of the priests of the pagan cult of Cybele which had its home in Galatia! The fierceness of this outburst is born of

Paul's passionate desire to keep the gospel free from all self-engendered additions which would denature it. 'Such a mutilation of the gospel stands for Paul on one and the same level as the most despicable pagan practices, by means of which men tried to assure themselves of the favour of the gods' (Ridderbos). [cf *Phil* 3.2: 'beware of the "mutilation" party' – Bruce.]

*V*13: **For ye, brethren, were called for freedom; only *use* not your freedom for an occasion to the flesh, but through love be servants one to another.**

For ye, brethren, were called for freedom; This verse echoes the challenge of 5.1, and like that verse it also marks a point of transition in the argument. 'For' looks back to *v* 12 and justifies the scorn poured on the Judaizers – 'for' *you* (emphatic) were not called for bondage but freedom! Yet this freedom, as Paul at once goes on to show, is not a liberty in licence, but the liberty of love [*vv* 13–26].

only *use* not your freedom for an occasion to the flesh, The qualification introduces an urgent warning. The Galatians must be on their guard against the abuse of this freedom, which would provide the flesh with a bridgehead that would allow sin to recapture lost ground. In this passage 'the flesh' has an ethical meaning, and 'it obviously signifies the depraved inclinations which are natural to man in his present state, and which, though subdued, are by no means extinguished even in the regenerate' (Brown).

but through love be servants one to another. Being free from the servitude of legalism, they are to regard themselves as bound by the claims of love. Forsaking the selfish individualism of lawless licence, they are constantly to seek the welfare of one another through that self-giving love which delights to express itself in mutual service.

*V*14: **For the whole law is fulfilled in one word,** *even* **in this: Thou shalt love thy neighbour as thyself.**

For the whole law has found its full expression in a single word, (Arndt-Gingrich) Paul's insistence that the law must find its proper expression in the life of believers is very striking when it is remembered that thus far the entire argument has been directed against the encroachments of legalism. With an unerring grasp of the principles at stake, he denounces the slavish spirit that vainly seeks justification by the law, while enjoining the fulfilment of the law by that love which is the fruit of faith. A similar thought is expressed in *Romans* 13.9, where the demands of the Decalogue are 'summed up' in this one word. 'Love, then, is both the *summary* (interpretive epitome or condensation) and the *realization in practice* of the entire God-given moral law, viewed as a unit' (Hendriksen).

even **in this: Thou shalt love thy neighbour as thyself.** It is significant that the apostle should enforce the abiding validity of the moral law by an appeal to a book which his opponents doubtless regarded as the stronghold of their ceremonialism [*Lev* 19.18]. Here '*love to God* is presupposed as the root from which *love to our neighbour* springs' (Fausset). All right believing in God is visibly reflected in right behaviour towards men [1 *John* 4.20, 21]. The skeleton of Christian doctrine is essential but this must be enfleshed by the living reality of Christian love, which is the love that *recognizes, considers,* and *cares* for the needs of our neighbour [cf *Luke* 10.25–37].[1]

*V*15: **But if ye bite and devour one another, take heed that ye be not consumed one of another.**

1. Cf L. H. Marshall, *The Challenge of New Testament Ethics*, pp. 106–107.

It seems reasonable to assume that it was no imaginary danger that called forth this strong warning. There was a tragic disparity between the obligation to fulfil the law by mutual love and the bitter dissensions about the law which prevailed among the Galatians and threatened to destroy their spiritual life. Let them take heed, for the moral savagery that delights to bite and devour could lead to nothing but mutual destruction. Even defenders of the truth must be careful about their spirit and manner in controversy.

V16: But I say, Walk by the Spirit, and ye shall not fulfil the lust of the flesh.

The Geneva Bible has the heading: *He sheweth them the battel betwixt the Spirit and the flesh; and the frutes of them bothe*. In these verses there is no hint of the 'Victorious Life' teaching of C. G. Trumbull, 'Let go and let God'.[1] On the contrary, the apostle's teaching is that all Christians are engaged in a constant warfare in which they are called to resist the unlawful demands of the 'flesh' by responding to the rightful claims of the 'Spirit'. To frustrate the desire of the 'flesh' believers are instructed to 'walk by the Spirit'. *They* are to do the walking, but they are to do it by the power of the Holy Spirit [*vv* 18, 25]. 'To be sure, we do not act in our own power, but only in so far as the Spirit graciously gives us power and ability to act. It is not as though the Spirit works partially in us, setting us in motion, whereupon we do the rest ... Rather, it is a balance in which the Spirit is completely sovereign and man is completely responsible: a hundred-hundred proposition, as contradictory as that may seem' (Edwin Palmer, *The Holy Spirit*, pp. 96, 179). 'Ye shall not fulfil' is the assurance that the flesh will fail to achieve the complete domination it desires [cf *v* 17b].

1. For an incisive criticism of this teaching, see Warfield's fine article 'The Victorious Life' in *Perfectionism*, pp. 349–399.

Intimations

Copies of "Life & Work" for August are a▸

<u>Tonight</u>: 7.00 Evening Worship. Preacher:

<u>Tuesday</u>: 8.00 pm Bible Study at Jean Kell▸

Reading: Galatians 1: v11 - ▸

<u>Wednesday</u>: Short Service at 12 noon, follo▸
of New Kilpatrick, the church will be open

6.30-7.30 pm Ministers' consultation▸

<u>Saturday</u>: NK Ramblers: (a) Beinn Chuirn,
noticeboard in Walkround.

<u>Next Sunday</u>: 10.30 am Morning Worship ▸

Preacher: The Reverend Neil MacG▸

7.00 pm Evening Worship.

Until Mr Symington returns on August 11, a▸
contact the Office (942 8827), Mr McIntyre▸
<u>Intimations for next Sunday by noon on Tu</u>▸
<u>Materials for the September "Breastplate" (i</u>▸
<u>Tony Brooke, by 8th August at latest!</u>

<u>Looking ahead</u> - Friday 10 September: FO▸
to all. Names on North Porch clipboard as▸
FONK 1994 calendars are on sale in the W▸
by surface mail.

*V*17: **For the flesh lusteth against the Spirit, and the Spirit against the flesh; for these are contrary the one to the other; that ye may not do the things that ye would.**

Unbelievers know nothing of the struggle depicted here, for is is only the Spirit who can prompt those desires which are contrary to the flesh. Hence 'Spirit' must refer to the Holy Spirit, 'for the human spirit in itself and unaided does not stand in direct antagonism to the flesh' (Lightfoot). Thus it is because the Spirit and the flesh are irreconcilably opposed to each other that there is a continual conflict going on within the believer.

so that ye cannot do the things that ye would. (AV) Is Paul here saying that the flesh prevents our complete obedience to the promptings of the Spirit, or that the presence of the Spirit enables us to resist the cravings of the flesh? In view of the assurance given in verse 16 it would seem that the latter meaning is preferable. 'To walk by the Spirit of God ensures that we do no longer as we please (*i.e.* fall to the false freedom of carnal impulse). Rather, we live in freedom which triumphs over such impulses. This is not freedom which steers an uncertain middle course between evil impulses and obedience to religious rules, but a new way which transcends them both' (Mikolaski).

*V*18: **But if ye are led by the Spirit, ye are not under the law.**

It is because believers are led by the Spirit that they are not under the law. As the Galatians experienced release from the curse and bondage of the law through receiving the Spirit in conversion, so victory over the flesh was to be experienced by the Spirit's inward leading and strengthening. Hence the privilege of being led by the Spirit also involved the duty of responding to that leading, which if resisted would rather ensure the ascendancy of the flesh [*Rom* 8.1–14]. 'If one is to offer resistance in the struggle between Spirit and flesh, one must be in the service of the Spirit and not in that of the law. That the demand of the law remains [*verse* 14] is not denied, of course. The issue, in short, is the strength, the power, that is necessary for the fulfilment of the law' (Ridderbos).

*V*19: **Now the works of the flesh are manifest, which are** *these*: **fornication, uncleanness, lasciviousness, 20 idolatry, sorcery, enmities, strife, jealousies, wraths, factions, divisions, parties, 21 envyings, drunkenness, revellings, and such like; of which I forewarn you, even as I did forewarn you, that they who practise such things shall not inherit the kingdom of God.**

Now the works of the flesh are manifest, 'The flesh concealed betrays itself by its own works, so that its discovery is easy ... *The works*, in the plural, because they are divided and often at variance, and even singly betray the flesh. But *the fruit*, being good, *verse* 22, is in the singular, because it is united and harmonious. Comp. *Eph* 5.11, 9' (Bengel).

which are: immorality, impurity, indecency, (Hendriksen) 1. *Sexual sins.* 'The flesh' is never made more manifest than it is by the besmirching and degrading sins of the flesh. Any society that begins by regarding them with indifference very shortly becomes enslaved by them. 'In nothing did early Christianity so thoroughly revolutionize the ethical standards of the pagan world as in regard to sexual relationships' (Duncan). Now that 'permissiveness' is an accepted norm, this note needs to be sounded again in no uncertain manner.

idolatry, sorcery, 2. *False religion.* Man in his rebellion against his Creator remains incurably religious, and he seeks to satisfy this instinct by making his own deities. He much prefers these lifeless puppets to the one true living God, because they allow him to pull the strings. In the same way magic is man's unlawful attempt to manipulate unseen spiritual forces to his own advantage. In an age which is not ostensibly religious, there has been a remarkable proliferation of false gods and a terrifying revival of occult arts and practices. Besides the parasitic growth of many new cults, the 'secular' gods of Communism, Scientism, and Humanism are worshipped with a fervour approaching religious ecstasy, while the increasing popularity of witchcraft, spiritism (alias Spiritualism), clairvoyance, astrology, and horoscopes heralds a relapse into the Dark Ages.

enmities, strife, jealousies, wraths, factions, divisions, parties, envyings, 3. *Sins of ill-will.* The largest group affords mournful proof of the depravity of the human heart [*Jer* 17.9]. Lightfoot sees an ascending scale in the arrangement of these 'violations of brotherly love'. Cherished 'enmities' lead to 'strife', which finds expression in 'outbreaks of jealousies', 'outbursts of anger', and 'unscrupulous intriguing'. These in turn lead to the point where the contending parties separate and form either temporary 'divisions' or permanent 'parties'. The final 'envyings' is 'a grosser breach of charity than any hitherto mentioned, the wish to deprive another of what he has' [cf *Prov* 14.30].

drunkenness, revellings, 4. *Intemperance.* To conclude Paul lists the sin of drunkenness and the revellings which are its natural accompaniment. 'Komos, the Revel, was made a god, and his rites were carried on quite systematically, and yet with all the ingenuity and inventiveness of the Greek mind, which lent perpetual novelty and variety to the revellings' (William Ramsay). And such orgiastic excesses are by no means unknown today!

and such like; This is by no means an exhaustive catalogue of the works of the flesh but only a representative list.

I warn you, as I warned you before, that those who do such things shall not inherit the kingdom of God. (RSV) The gospel Paul preached was no form of cheap and easy believism, for it demanded and provided for the radical reformation of the whole life. In dealing with pagan Gentiles who were ignorant of the moral law, the apostle was always careful to warn them of the fatal consequences of continuing in sin that grace may abound [*Rom* 6 1ff]. Here he again reminds the Galatians that those who deny Christ's present reign of grace by their persistence in such sins shall not inherit the kingdom of God at the end of the age [cf 1 *Cor* 6.9, 10].

*V*22: **But the fruit of the Spirit is love, joy, peace, long-suffering, kindness, goodness, faithfulness, 23 meekness, self-control; against such there is no law.**

But the fruit of the Spirit Of a very different character is that supernatural 'fruit' whose *organic development* springs from the one living root of the Spirit [cf *John* 15.4, 5]. This 'fruit' includes 'those ethical qualities and spiritual experiences which were not popularly thought of as evidences of the Spirit's presence, but which, to the mind of Paul, were of far greater value than the so-called *charismata*. See 1 *Cor*, chaps 12–14, especially 12.31, chap 13, and 14.1' (Burton). The harvest of the Spirit falls into three triads which may be roughly classified as follows: 1. *Spiritual graces*; 2. *Social conduct*; 3. *Personal discipline*.

is love, The greatest Christian grace appropriately heads the list. Love is the animating principle 'of all the other graces – greater than faith and hope, for "God is love"; love to God and all that bears his image, being the essence of the first and second tables of the law, – all the other graces being at length absorbed by it as the flower is lost in the fruit. 1 *Cor* 13; *Rom* 12.9' (Eadie).

joy, This is not *joie de vivre*, the mere feeling of physical well-being. It is a spiritual joy that is not extinguished by the most adverse circumstances. So Paul and Silas, though beaten and in prison, sang hymns to God at midnight [*Acts* 16.25]. The ultimate object of all Christian preaching is to bring men that joy which is unattainable by any other means [*John* 15.11]. As Raymond Stamm points out, next to Paul's letters, this spirit of joy which is brought forth by the gospel is nowhere better illustrated than in Luke's writings [e.g. *Luke* 2.10, 15.10, 24.52; *Acts* 5.41, 8.8, 8.39, 13.48, 52, 15.31].

peace, The primary reference here is to the believer's assurance of peace with God through faith in Christ; it is the blessing of a conscience that has been pacified by the knowledge that Christ has satisfied all the claims of divine justice on its behalf [*Rom* 5.1]. The Galatians must learn that to doubt the sufficiency of Christ's sacrifice is to lose all sense of peace with God, for the conscience can find its rest in no other doctrine but this. But no outward storms can disturb the inward calm of those who are guarded by the 'peace of God, which passeth all understanding' [*Phil* 4.7].

longsuffering, 'The word means "long-temperedness" and refers to the endurance of wrong and exasperating conduct on the part of others without flying into a rage or passionately desiring vengeance. One of the great ethical qualities of God celebrated in Holy Scripture is that He is "slow to anger", and Paul here suggests that the spiritual man shares in this characteristic of God' (L. H. Marshall).

[113]

kindness, As God is kind even to the unthankful and the evil [*Luke* 6.35], so believers are to reflect the divine kindness by treating others in the way God has treated them [*Eph* 4.32].

goodness, This is the goodness that *benefits* others even as Christ 'went about doing good' [*Acts* 10.38]. Thus in this triad which deals with the believer's relations with his fellow-men we have another ascending scale: 'longsuffering' is *passive*, 'patient endurance under injuries inflicted by others'; 'kindness', *neutral*, 'kindly disposition towards one's neighbours' not necessarily taking a practical form; 'goodness', *active*, 'goodness, beneficence' as an energetic principle (Lightfoot).

faithfulness, 'It is clear from the subordinate place assigned to *pistis* that it does not here denote the cardinal grace of faith in God which is the root of all religion, but rather good faith in dealing with men, and due regard to their just claims' (Rendall).

meekness, This is not spineless weakness, but the gentleness of a strength which has been brought under control, as a horse is made obedient to bit and bridle. As meekness is thus the mark of the man who has been mastered by God [*Num* 12.3], so the secret of all effective service is found in willing submission to Christ's yoke [*Matt* 11.29, 30].

self-control; This is the grace which gives victory over the desires of the flesh [*v* 16]. It is a virtue that is exercised by the Christian and which produces in him the desire to 'bring into captivity every thought to the obedience of Christ'. Thereby he 'escapes the corruption that is in the world by lust'. [2 *Cor.* 10.5; 2 *Pet.* 1.4]

against such there is no law. While law, whether written or unwritten, must condemn the works of the flesh, all these graces, and others like them, are condemned by no law. In fact, as the fruit of the Spirit, they are in principle a fulfilling of the law's demand [*v* 14]. Thus, 'where the Spirit reigns, the law has no longer any dominion. By moulding our hearts to His own righteousness, the Lord delivers us from the severity of the law, so that He does not deal with us according to its covenant, nor does He bind our consciences under its condemnation. Yet the law continues to perform its office of teaching and exhorting. But the Spirit of adoption sets us free from subjection to it' (Calvin). [*v* 18; 1 *Tim* 1.9]

*V*24: **And they that are of Christ Jesus have crucified the flesh with the passions and the lusts thereof.**

And those who belong to Christ Jesus have crucified the flesh with its passions and desires. (RSV) Paul is reminding the Galatians of the moment in their experience when they made a definitive break with the flesh and its sinful desires. In their conversion they made this radical breach with sin by identifying themselves with the Christ who was crucified to secure their release from the dominion of the flesh. This 'does not mean that since that moment the flesh can no longer bring an influence to bear, but rather that its corruptness is acknowledged and is assigned to death, not by the cross of Christ alone, but by the believers themselves also' (Ridderbos). As they then recognized that the flesh was crucified with Christ, so now they must put to death its passions and desires as having no longer any right to live.

*V*25: **If we live by the Spirit, by the Spirit let us also walk.**

'Walk' here means to walk in line, and 'may imply a more studied following of a prescribed course' (Ellicott). Calvin's fine comment on this verse shows that it was not without reason that Warfield called him 'the theologian of the Holy Spirit'. He says, 'Now in his usual way, Paul draws an exhortation out of the doctrine. The death of the flesh is the life of the Spirit. If God's Spirit lives in us, let Him govern all our actions. There will always be many who impudently boast of living in the Spirit, but Paul challenges them to prove their claim. As the soul does not live idly in the body, but gives motion and vigour to every member and part, so the Spirit of God cannot dwell in us without manifesting Himself by the outward effects. By "life" is here meant the inward power, and by "walk", the outward actions. Paul means that works are witnesses to spiritual life'.

V26: Let us not become vainglorious, provoking one another, envying one another.

Walking by the Spirit must quench the natural tendency to turn spiritual privileges into an occasion for boasting, by which fellow-believers are provoked to envy the assumed pre-eminence. In this exhortation Paul may have had the situation in Galatia very much in mind [v15], but the vainglorying he deprecates is not to be limited by it. 'Experience of the mission-field and of religious "revivals" reveals how prone it is to arise where the emphasis on the life of the Spirit has not yet led to a realization of its ethical implications. Paul has often to warn his churches against it [cf notably Phil 2.1 ff]' (Duncan). The exhortation has an intimate bearing on what follows.

CHAPTER SIX

Paul exhorts the Galatians to restore those who fall, and to bear one another's burdens [vv 1–5]. They should support their teachers liberally, and are not to become weary in well-doing, for in due season they shall reap what they have sown [vv 6–10]. In a final warning against the Judaizers he contrasts their selfish motives with the self-denying love which springs from an interest in Christ crucified [vv 11–16]. He enforces this appeal by reminding them of his own sufferings, and closes the Epistle with the benediction [vv 17, 18].

V_1: **Brethren, even if a man be overtaken in any trespass, ye who are spiritual, restore such a one in a spirit of gentleness; looking to thyself, lest thou also be tempted.**

My brothers, if one of your number is caught off his guard by some sin, those among you who are spiritual men must restore him in a spirit of gentleness. (Bruce) Mindful of man's frailty and Satan's subtlety, Paul recognizes that not all who seek to walk by the Spirit will always do so without stumbling. In such cases, those who are noted for their consistent obedience to the Spirit's leading [5.16, 18, 25] must gently restore their fallen brother. The word 'restore' shows that this is no task for the spiritually inexperienced. It is used to describe the work that calls for special skill, e.g.

setting a broken limb, and mending nets [*Matt* 4.21]. 'To "restore such an one", is to use the appropriate means of convincing him of his error and sin, and bringing him back to the path of truth and righteousness' (Brown).

looking to thyself, lest thou also be tempted. A striking transition from the plural to the singular. Each of you must watch *himself*, for none is immune from temptation. Therefore a censorious spirit is out of place in those who are subject to the same weaknesses [*Matt* 7.2–5].

V2: **Bear ye one another's burdens, and so fulfil the law of Christ.**

The primary reference is to the duty of sharing the spiritual burdens by which fellow-believers are oppressed, though other burdens are not excluded (compare for example *v* 6). The precept is well illustrated by Chrysostom: 'He who is quick and irritable, let him bear with the slow and the sluggish; and let the slow, in his turn, bear with the impetuosity of his fiery brother: each knowing that the burden is heavier to him who bears it than to him who bears with it'. Paul sees in this mutual burden-bearing the active manifestation of the love that fulfils the law of Christ. Against the legalism that would seek to fulfil the law in its own strength, Paul sees the capacity to fulfil that same law as being given to believers by Christ through the Spirit [5.16]. As Ridderbos says, 'The new element is not the content of the law, although Christ's coming and His work modified it, but in the root of obedience, namely, Christ'.

V3: **For if a man thinketh himself to be something when he is nothing, he deceiveth himself.**

'For' indicates the close connection with the previous verse. Self-importance 'based on self-ignorance is the grand hindrance to the duty of mutual burden-bearing. If a man thinks himself so perfect that he can have no burden which others may carry with him, or for him; if he regards himself so far above frailty, sin, or sorrow, that he neither needs nor expects sympathy nor help, – he will not readily stoop to bear the burdens of others' (Eadie). Such an one is sadly self-deceived for the flattering estimate he entertains of himself has no basis in reality. He believes he is something, when in fact he is nothing!

*V*4: **But let each man prove his own work, and then shall he have his glorying in regard of himself alone, and not of his neighbour.**

But let each one test his own work; then his reason to boast will be in himself alone, and not in (comparing himself with) someone else. (Hendriksen) 'It is not what we gain by detracting from others, but what we have without any comparison, that is truly praiseworthy' (Calvin). Instead of indulging the Pharisaic pride which exalts self by looking down on others, each is to bring his own work to the test [*Luke* 18.11]. This is all he is qualified to do, since this self-knowledge cannot be applied as a standard to test another's work [2 *Cor* 10.2]. Every man is to find the basis for boasting in himself, for he alone knows what God's grace has wrought in his life. Hence his glorying will be a glorying in the Lord [*v* 14; 1 *Cor* 1.31].

*V*5: **For each man shall bear his own burden.**

For each person will have to bear his own load. (Hendriksen) Or 'shoulder his own pack' (J. B. Phillips). The thought again follows on from the preceding verse: 'everyone is to concern himself about his own burden, rather than to compare himself complacently with others' (Arndt-Gingrich).

For each has his own burden of sin and weakness which ought to lead him to be charitable towards others. The word used here 'was applied to the pack usually carried by a porter or soldier on the march ... It is necessary to distinguish this from the heavy loads to which verse 2 refers as needing the help of Christian brethren for the relief of overtaxed carriers' (Rendall).

*V*6: **But let him that is taught in the word communicate unto him that teacheth in all good things.**

Let him who is taught the word share all good things with him who teaches. (RSV) This is probably to be connected with verse 2: 'I spoke of bearing one another's burdens. There is one special application I would make of this rule. Provide for the temporal wants of your teachers in Christ' (Lightfoot). In pagan religion there were *priests* who levied dues on the sacrifices they offered, but no *teachers* who would have had to rely on a system of voluntary contributions for their support. 'Hence the duty of supporting teachers or preachers had to be continually impressed upon the attention of all Paul's converts from Paganism. The tendency to fail in it was practically universal; it was connected with a universal fact in contemporary society; perhaps it was not unconnected with a universal characteristic of human nature' (Ramsay). [cf 1 *Cor* 9.11f; 1 *Tim* 5.17f] It was not pagan ritual that changed the ancient world, but the communication of a message which demanded the understanding of faith and issued in a moral transformation of the character. An *ex opere operato* faith, whether heathen or 'Christian', is always an ethically sterile thing.

*V*7: **Be not deceived; God is not mocked: for whatsoever a man soweth, that shall he also reap.**

God is not mocked 'That of which the apostle speaks is not a ridicule of God which he will not leave unpunished, but an outwitting of God, an evasion of his laws which men think to accomplish, but, in fact, can not' (Burton). This stern warning sums up the appeal of the whole letter. Let the Galatian fascination for law find a healthy outlet in the contemplation of this immutable law of God's moral government! Although the seeds of legalism may be fair in the blade, they shall not fail of their appointed reward. Full maturity will reveal a fruitlessness that must be swept down by the avenging sickle of divine wrath. Men are the dupes of their own sinful self-love, believing that what they regard as a truism in the natural world has no application in the spiritual realm. On the contrary, the forthcoming harvest will inexorably reveal the value or otherwise of what has been sown in the present life and vindicate the justice of the respective judgments they call forth [5.19–23]. For the equity of the law of sowing and reaping is manifestly beyond reproach.

*V*8: **For he that soweth unto his own flesh shall of the flesh reap corruption; but he that soweth unto the Spirit shall of the Spirit reap eternal life.**

That God is not mocked when men deceive themselves is shown by the fact that the future life only brings to fruition the seed sown here. 'Unto his own flesh' indicates that sin is no alien principle coming to man from without, but is entirely *natural* to him and is essentially *selfish* in its aims. Hence the man who sows 'unto his own flesh' with a view to fulfilling its desires must of the flesh reap 'corruption' [cf 1 *Cor* 3.17; 2 *Pet* 2.12]. This is to experience 'eternal destruction from the face of the Lord' [2 *Thess* 1.9], and is the opposite of 'eternal life' [*v* 8b]. Thus the term 'corruption' shows that this awful infliction of divine wrath is 'not an *arbitrary* punishment of fleshly-mindedness, but is its *natural* fruit' (Fausset). [cf *Rom* 8.12, 13].

On the other hand, he who sows 'unto the Spirit' (i.e. who obediently follows the leading of the author of his spiritual life) shall reap the harvest of eternal life from the selfsame Spirit [*Rom* 8.11]. The function of the Holy Spirit in the future life is twofold. He is the source of resurrection-life and the 'element' in which it shall be lived. 'He produces the event and in continuance underlies the state which is the result of it. He is Creator and Sustainer at once, the *Creator Spiritus* and the Sustainer of the supernatural state of the future life in one' (Geerhardus Vos, *The Pauline Eschatology*, p. 163).

*V*9: **And let us not be weary in well-doing: for in due season we shall reap, if we faint not.**

And let us not lose heart (Arndt-Gingrich) Paul now presents the Galatians with the grand incentive to unwearied perseverance in well-doing: 'we shall reap, if we faint not'. 'The great cause of weariness in well-doing is a deficiency in faith, and a corresponding undue influence of present and sensible things ... Nothing is so much calculated to produce languor as a suspicion that all our exertions are likely to be fruitless; and nothing is better fitted to dispel it than the assurance that they shall assuredly be crowned with success' (Brown). [1 *Cor* 15.58]

*V*10: **So then, as we have opportunity, let us work that which is good toward all men, and especially toward them that are of the household of the faith.**

We have now the 'season' for *sowing*, as there will be hereafter the 'due season' [*v* 9] for *reaping*. In one sense the whole of life is the season of opportunity; and in a narrower sense, there occur in it especially convenient seasons. The latter are lost in looking for 'still more convenient seasons [*Acts* 24.25]. We shall not always have the opportunity "we have" now. Satan is sharpened to the greater zeal in evil-doing by the shortness of his time [*Rev* 12.12]. Let us be sharpened to the greater zeal in well-doing by the shortness of ours' (Fausset).

and especially toward them that are of the household of the faith. As every right-minded man does well to his own family [*1 Tim* 5.8], so believers must do the same to those who belong to the household of the faith – i.e. those who are made members of God's household in virtue of their faith in Christ [*Eph* 2.19].

*V*11: **See with how large letters I write unto you with mine own hand.**

This verse marks the point at which Paul takes up the pen from his amanuensis to write the final admonition in his own hand. By these large letters he would impress upon the Galatians the supreme importance of remaining faithful to the gospel of God's redeeming grace in which Christ is set forth as the sinner's all-sufficient Saviour. 'The boldness of the handwriting answers to the force of the Apostle's convictions. The size of the characters will arrest the attention of his readers in spite of themselves' (Lightfoot).

*V*12: **As many as desire to make a fair show in the flesh, they compel you to be circumcised; only that they may not be persecuted for the cross of Christ.**

It was not because the Judaizers were genuinely concerned for the spiritual welfare of the Galatians that they pressed them to receive circumcision, but because they desired 'to make a fair show in the flesh'. It was in the sphere of 'the flesh' (the body) that this fleshly (non-spiritual) glorying showed itself. Their unspiritual mind was revealed by their preoccupation with a specious outward show. 'The whole expression describes those to whom it refers as desiring to stand well in matters whose real basis is physical rather than spiritual' (Burton).

The Jews were implacably opposed to the preaching of the cross, for it offered the Gentiles salvation without obliging them to become Jewish proselytes, thus destroying their religious pre-eminence by placing them on a level with the Gentile world. To escape this enmity the Judaizers compromised the gospel by insisting that Gentile converts should submit to circumcision in token of their allegiance to the law. As the missionaries of a Jewish ecumenism, tolerated alike by pagan Rome and unbelieving Jerusalem, these Judaizers therefore adroitly avoided the scandal of the cross. 'But this syncretistic mixture of law and gospel veiled the cross and its salvation, so free and fitting to mankind without distinction of race or blood; so that their profession was deceptive, perilous in its consequences, and prompted and shaped by an ignoble and cowardly selfishness; it was a "fair show", but only in the sphere of fleshly things, and assumed on purpose to avoid persecution' (Eadie).

V13: For not even they who receive circumcision do themselves keep the law; but they desire to have you circumcised, that they may glory in your flesh.

These zealous advocates for circumcision do not themselves feel bound by the yoke they were asking others to accept, for like all hypocrites they were motivated by purely external considerations [cf Matt 23.4]. Although they honoured the law with their lips, they showed no corresponding concern to obey it in their lives, and the only reason they desired to impose this outward mark upon the Gentiles was to make them members of their party. All their powers of persuasion were directed to this end in order that their glorying in a Gentile surrender to a carnal rite might transform the fanatical opposition of the Jews to the gospel into a complacent acceptance of their activities.

V14: **But far be it from me to glory, save in the cross of our Lord Jesus Christ, through which the world hath been crucified unto me, and I unto the world.**

In emphatic contrast with the boasting of the Judaizers, which has its sphere and basis in the mere material flesh of men, the apostle sets forth as *his* ground of boasting, the central fact of his gospel, the cross of Christ [cf 1 *Cor* 1.18 ff]. '*The world* as used here is an epitome of everything outside of Christ in which man seeks his glory and puts his trust' (Ridderbos). It is through the cross that the world has been crucified unto Paul, and he unto the world. This instrument of his union with Christ was also the symbol of his separation from the world. So that in his reckoning the world was as dead to him, as he was in the estimation of the world. If the world now had nothing but contempt for him, it was because it recognized that he no longer belonged to it as he once did [2.20]. 'Men to whom the world is not crucified, are certainly not believers; and men professing Christianity, who are not "crucified to the world" – men whom the world loves and honours, – have cause to stand in doubt themselves. Where the Cross holds the place in the heart which it did in the apostle's, and exercises the influence over the character and conduct it did in him, it will be equally clear that the world is crucified to the individual, and he to the world' (Brown).

V15: **For neither is circumcision anything, nor uncircumcision, but a new creature.**

Since nothing external can effect a saving change in man, his outward state is a matter of indifference; circumcision is no help and uncircumcision is no hindrance [5.6]. Man's need can only be met by a 'new creation' (ASV margin). 'The spiritual renewal springs out of living union to Christ, and it is everything. For it re-enstamps the image of God on the soul, and restores it to its pristine felicity and fellowship. It is not external – neither a change of opinion, party, or outer life. Nor is it a change in the essence or organization of the soul, but in its inner being – in its springs of thought and feeling, in its powers and motives – by the Spirit of God and the influence of the truth. "All old things pass away; behold, all things are become new", 2 *Cor* 5.17. This creation is "new" – new in its themes of thought, in its susceptibilities of enjoyment, and in its spheres of energy; it finds itself in a new world, into which it is ushered by a new birth' (Eadie).

*V*16: **And as many as shall walk by this rule, peace** *be* **upon them, and mercy, and upon the Israel of God.**

And as many as shall walk by this rule, peace (be) upon them and mercy, even upon the Israel of God. (Hendriksen) It is upon as many as shall walk by this rule, and not upon as many as desire to make a fair show in the flesh [*v* 12], that the peace and mercy of God shall rest. Such blessings are exclusive to the new Israel of God, even to those who have found a new standard of life in Christ. For only those thus quickened by Christ are able to 'walk in newness of life' [cf *Rom* 8.1, 2]. 'Those who walk by the rule of the spirit are declared to be indeed the true Israel of God, not the Jews who have the name of Israel, but are really only the children of Abraham after the flesh' (Rendall). [3.29; *Phil* 3.3].

*V*17: **Henceforth let no man trouble me; for I bear branded on my body the marks of Jesus.**

Henceforth let no man trouble me; for I bear on my body the marks of Jesus. (RSV) Paul is confident that he will hear no more of the empty pretensions of the Judaizers, for he bears on his body the marks of what it cost him to bring the gospel to the Galatians [cf *Acts* 14.19]. The suggestion that the expression is borrowed from the pagan practice of branding slaves or of religious tattooing is wholly inappropriate to an apostle of Christ. 'The scars on Paul's body belonged to Jesus, were like the wounds he himself suffered, for Paul's scars were truly suffered because of Christ. Compare 2 *Cor* 1.5; 4.10; *Col* 1.24. A far later age invented "stigmata of Jesus", a reproduction of the marks of the five wounds in the hands, the feet, and the side of Jesus. These "stigmata" are either violent pains in these parts of the body or marks that turn red and, in some cases, bleed. All of these peculiar phenomena are pathological and have nothing to do with Paul's scars' (Lenski).

*V*18: **The grace of our Lord Jesus Christ be with your spirit, brethren. Amen.**

Apart from the solemn 'Amen', 'so let it be', 'brethren' is Paul's last word to the Galatians. It is at once a word of affection and appeal. He accounts them as his brethren still, and has confidence that their future conduct will justify this address. 'He prays not only that grace may be bestowed upon them freely, but that they may have a proper feeling of it in their minds. It is only really enjoyed by us when it reaches to our spirit. We ought therefore to ask that God would prepare in our souls a habitation for His grace. Amen.' (Calvin).

Soli Deo Gloria

BIBLIOGRAPHY

Alford, Henry, *The Greek Testament* (Rivingtons, 1865)

Allis, Oswald T., *Revision or New Translation?* (Presbyterian & Reformed, 1948)

Arndt, W. F. – Gingrich, F. W., *A Greek-English Lexicon of the New Testament* (University of Chicago Press, 1957)

Bengel, J. A., *New Testament Word Studies* (Kregel, 1971)

Boice, James Montgomery, *Galatians* (EBC) (Pickering & Inglis, 1976)

Brown, John, *Exposition of Galatians* (Sovereign Grace Book Club, 1957)

Bruce, F. F., *An Expanded Paraphrase on the Epistles of Paul* (Paternoster, 1965)

Bruce, F. F., *New Testament History* (Nelson, 1969)

Bruce, F. F., *Tradition Old and New* (Paternoster, 1970)

Bruner, Frederick Dale, *A Theology of the Holy Spirit* (Hodder & Stoughton, 1971)

Burton, Ernest De Witt, *Galatians* (ICC) (T. & T. Clark, 1921)

Calvin, John, *Galatians – Colossians* (The Saint Andrew Press, 1965) (Translated by T. H. L. Parker)

Cole, R. A., *Galatians – Introduction and Commentary* (TNTC) (Tyndale, 1965)

Denney, James, *The Death of Christ* (Tyndale, 1964)

Duncan, George S., *Galatians* (MNTC) (Hodder & Stoughton, 1934)

Eadie, John, *Galatians* (Zondervan, nd)

Ellicott, Charles J., *Galatians* (Longmans, Green, 1867)

Fausset, A. R., *Galatians* (JFB) (Collins, 1874)

Fergusson, James, *A Brief Exposition of the Epistles of Paul* (The Banner of Truth Trust, 1978)

Findlay, G. G., *Galatians* (EB) (Hodder & Stoughton, 1888)

Guthrie, Donald, *Galatians* (NCB) (Nelson, 1969)

Guthrie, Donald, *New Testament Introduction* (Tyndale, 1970)

Hendriksen, William, *Galatians* (NTC) (The Banner of Truth Trust, 1969)

Henry, Matthew, *Commentary on the Holy Bible* (various editions)

Hoeksema, Herman, *Reformed Dogmatics* (Reformed Free Publishing, 1966)

Jeremias, Joachim, *The Prayers of Jesus* (SCM, 1967)

Kittel, G. – Friedrich, G., *Theological Dictionary of the New Testament* Vols. 1–10 (Eerdmans, 1964–1976) (Translated by Geoffrey W. Bromiley: Index by Ronald E. Pitkin)

Ladd, George Eldon, *A Theology of the New Testament* (Eerdmans 1974)

Ladd, George Eldon, contributor to *Apostolic History and the Gospel* (Paternoster, 1970)

Lenski, R. C. H., *The Interpretation of Galatians* (Augsburg, 1961)

Lightfoot, J. B., *Galatians* (Zondervan, 1962)

Luther, Martin, *Lectures on Galatians, 1519, 1535* (Concordia, 1963–64)

McDonald, H. D., *Freedom in Faith* (Pickering & Inglis, 1973)

Machen, J. Gresham, *The New Testament* (The Banner of Truth Trust, 1976) (Edited by W. John Cook)

Machen, J. Gresham, *Christianity and Liberalism* (Victory Press, nd)

Marshall, L. H., *The Challenge of New Testament Ethics* (Macmillan, 1946)

Mayor, J. B., *The Epistle of James* (Zondervan, nd)

Mikolaski, Samuel J., *Galatians* (NBC-Revised) (IVP, 1970)

Moffatt, James, *Love in the New Testament* (Hodder & Stoughton, 1929)

Murray, John, *Redemption Accomplished and Applied* (The Banner of Truth Trust, 1961)

Packer, J. I., contributor to *The New Bible Dictionary* (IVP, 1962)

Palmer, Edwin H., *The Holy Spirit* (Presbyterian & Reformed, 1964)

Perkins, William, *Commentarie on Galatians* (London, 1617)

Poole, Matthew, *Commentary on the Holy Bible* (The Banner of Truth Trust, 1963)

Ramsay, William M., *Historical Commentary on the Epistle to the Galatians* (Hodder & Stoughton, 1900)

BIBLIOGRAPHY

Rendall, Frederic, *Galatians* (EGT) (Eerdmans, 1974)

Ridderbos, Hermann, *Galatians* (NLC) (Marshall, Morgan & Scott, 1954)

Ridderbos, Herman N., *Paul and Jesus* (Presbyterian & Reformed, 1957)

Robertson, A. T., *Word Pictures in the New Testament* Vol. IV (Broadman, 1931)

Skilton, John H., *Machen's Notes on Galatians* (Presbyterian and Reformed, 1972)

Stamm, Raymond T., *The Epistle to the Galatians* (IB) (Abingdon, 1953)

Stott, John R. W., *Only One Way* (IVP, 1973)

Trapp, John, *Commentary on the New Testament* (Sovereign Grace Book Club, 1958)

Vine, W. E., *An Expository Dictionary of New Testament Words* (Oliphants, 1958)

Vos, Geerhardus, *Biblical Theology* (The Banner of Truth Trust, 1975)

Vos, Geerhardus, *Pauline Eschatology* (Eerdmans, 1961)

Warfield, B. B., *Calvin and Augustine* (Presbyterian & Reformed, 1956)

Warfield, B. B., *Perfectionism* (Presbyterian & Reformed, 1958)

Warfield, B. B., *The Inspiration and Authority of the Bible* (Marshall, Morgan & Scott, 1959)

Williams, A. Lukyn, *Galatians* (CGT) (CUP, 1910)

Young, E. J., *Thy Word is Truth* (The Banner of Truth Trust, 1963)